IN MY
MOTHER'S GARDEN

IN MY MOTHER'S GARDEN

by The Vanessa–Ann Collection

Meredith® Press
New York, New York

With a huge,
heartfelt thank you
to our
two dear friends
whose energy and vitality,
imagination and affection
have made
our lives so much more
than they
ever could have been.

Dear Crafter,

Thank you for selecting *In My Mother's Garden*. Within this book you'll find a charming collection of garden designs in a variety of cross-stitch projects. From rose petals to vegetables, the projects cover every step as you meander among the colorful blooms in "your mother's garden."

We at Meredith® Press strive to bring you the very highest quality craft books, with original designs, clear, easy-to-follow charts, patterns, and instructions. Each project is photographed in full color to help provide easy reference and inspiration for each project you stitch.

We are proud to publish *In My Mother's Garden*, and we hope you'll enjoy using it to create your own projects.

Sincerely,

Heidi Kaisand

Heidi Kaisand
Editorial Project Manager

For Meredith® Press

Meredith® Press is an imprint of Meredith® Books:
President, Book Group: Joseph J. Ward
Vice President, Editorial Director: Elizabeth P. Rice
Executive Editor: Connie Schrader
Editorial Project Manager: Heidi Kaisand
Production Manager: Bill Rose

For Chapelle Ltd.

Owners: Terrece Beesley and Jo Packham
Staff: Trice Boerens, Tina Annette Brady, Sandra Durbin Chapman, Holly Fuller, Kristi Glissmeyer, Susan Jorgensen, Margaret Shields Marti, Jackie McCowen, Barbara Milburn, Lisa Miles, Pamela Randall, Jennifer Roberts, Florence Stacey, Nancy Whitley, Gloria Zirkel.

Designers: Trice Boerens, Terrece Beesley

Photographer: Ryne Hazen

The photographs in this book were taken at Mary Gaskill's Trends and Traditions, Ogden UT; Anita Louise's Bearlace Cottage, Park City UT; Edie Stockstill's home, Salt Lake City UT and RC Willey Furniture, Salt Lake City UT. Their friendly cooperation and trust are deeply appreciated.

ISBN: 0-696-02376-8
Library of Congress: 92–085379
First Printing 1992

Published by Meredith® Press

Distributed by Meredith® Corporation, Des Moines IA.

10 9 8 7 6 5 4 3

Printed in the United States of America.

Garden of Letters   6
   Precious Rose   18
   Clever Hideaway   19
   Luminous Roses   22
   Rose Tray   23

You Lift Me Up   26
   Framed Fancy   33
   Keeping Secrets   36
   Jewelry Keeper   40
   Butterfly Wings   42

Magnolia Ladies   44
   Pocket Full O' Flowers   53
   Little Lights   56
   Prissy Pillow   58

In My Mother's Garden   60
   Wings on Air Afghan   68
   Garden Gazebo   72

Mother's Favorite Saying   74
   Home Tweet Home   83
   Fresh Carrots   86
   Cozy Coaster Basket   88

The Peaceful Pasture   92
   Soft Wings   102
   Meadow Reflections   104
   Enduring Lily   108

Counting Dinosaur   110
   Fat Red Hen   118
   Mother's Memories   120
   Cowpoke Star   120

Molly, Plain and Fancy   124
   Doll Body   126
   Basic Dress   128
   Petticoat   128
   Pantaloons   128
   Roses and Bows   130
   Spring Fancy   132
   Learning the ABCs   134
   Peachy Peas   136
   Dino Dynamite   138
   Country Maid   140

General Instructions   141
Suppliers   143
Index   144

One of Mother's gardens is a treasure-house of fragrant blossoms, freshly cut and still sparkling with morning dew. Her other garden, a warm memory of home and love, is a treasure-house of knowledge. In it, a simple alphabet, learned at her knee, opens a new world as lovely and inspiring as a bouquet of roses.

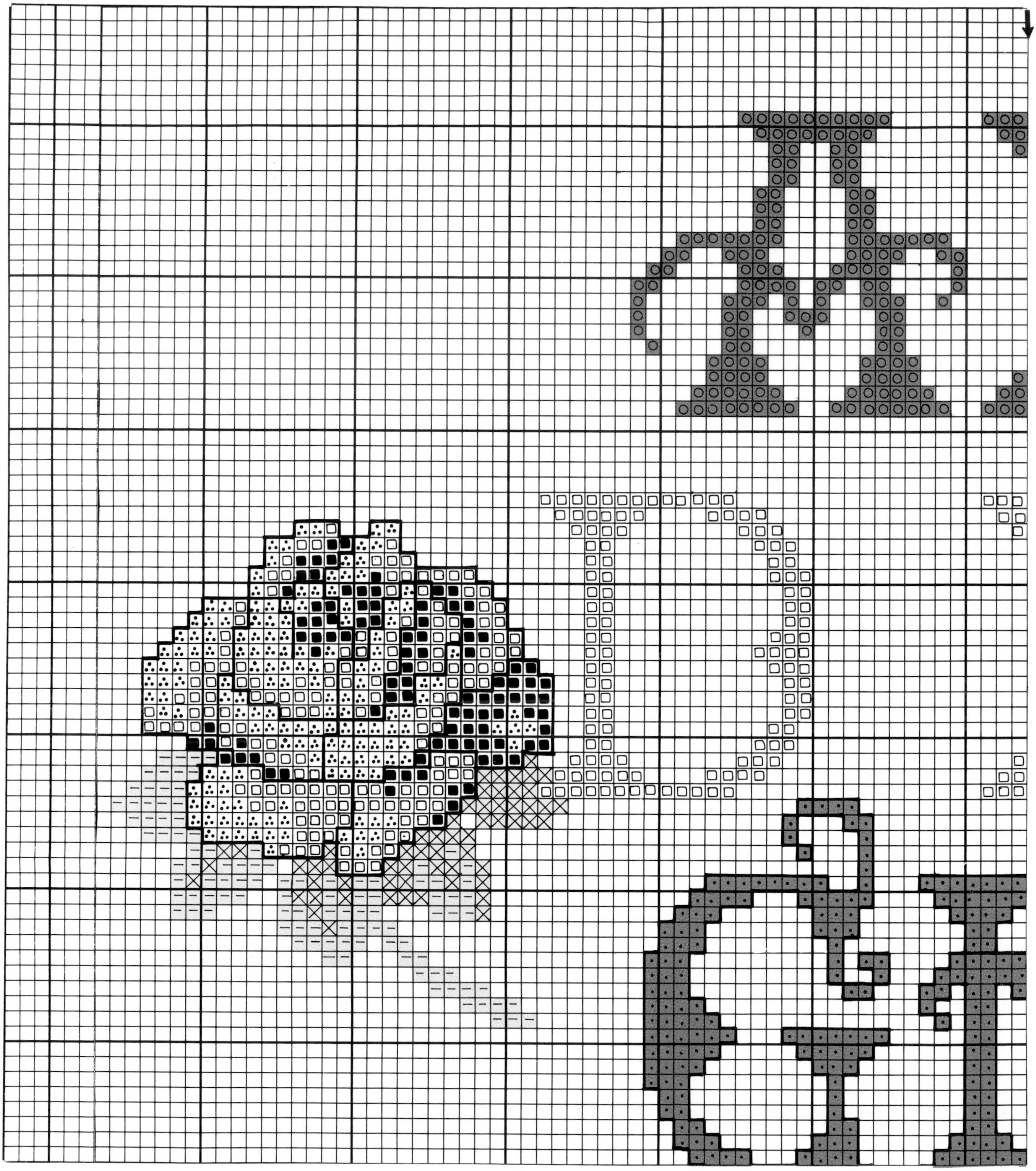

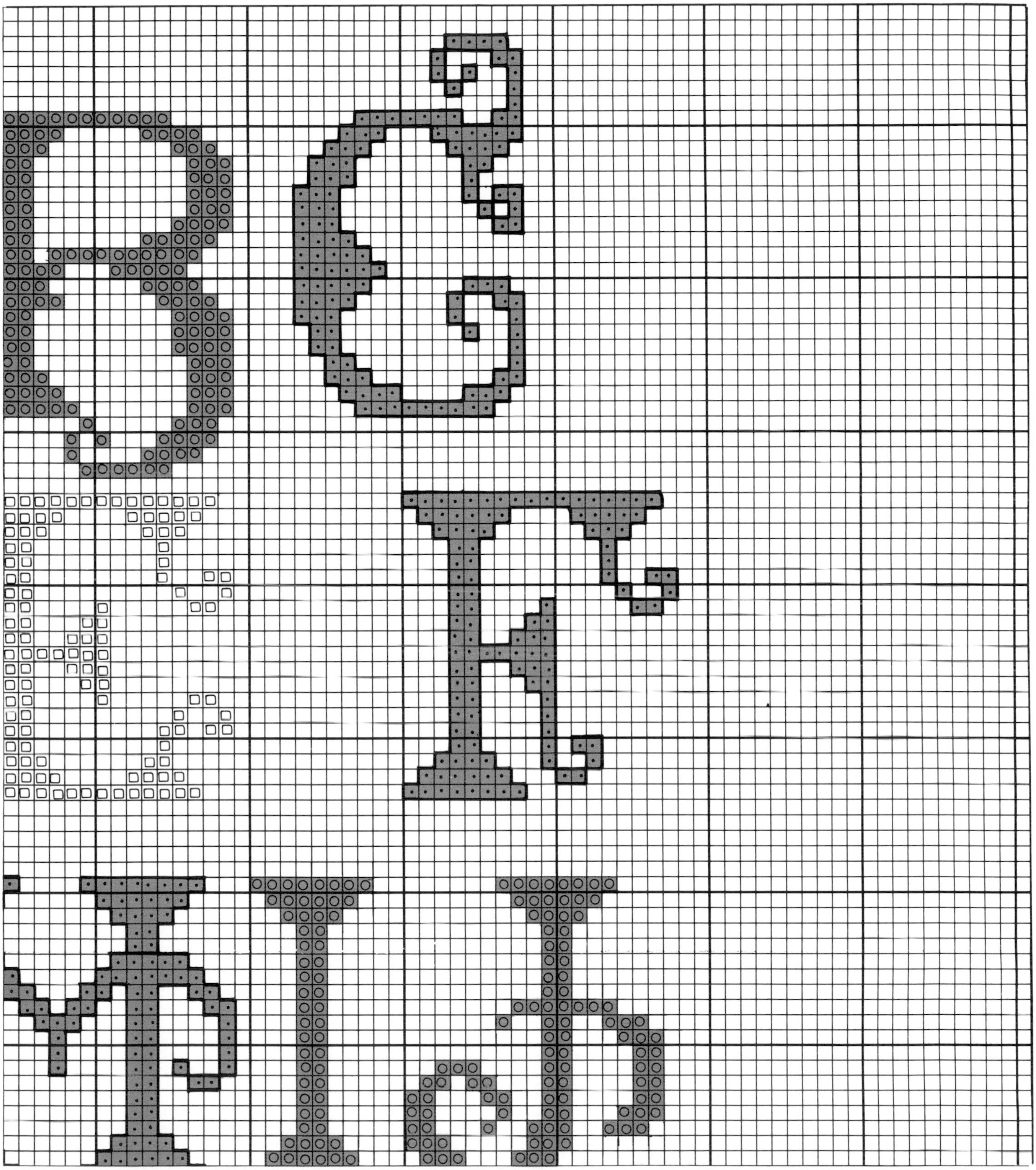

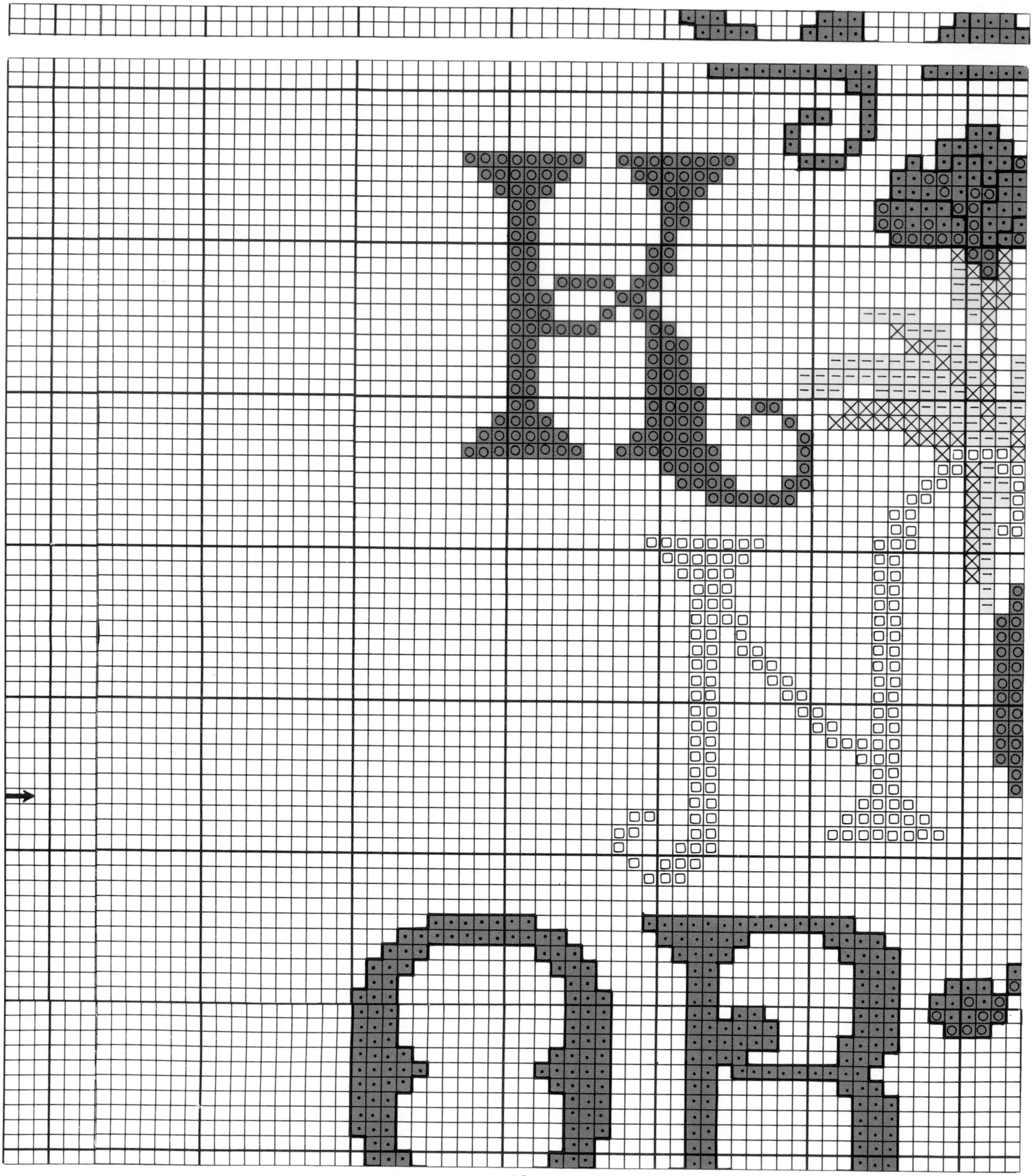

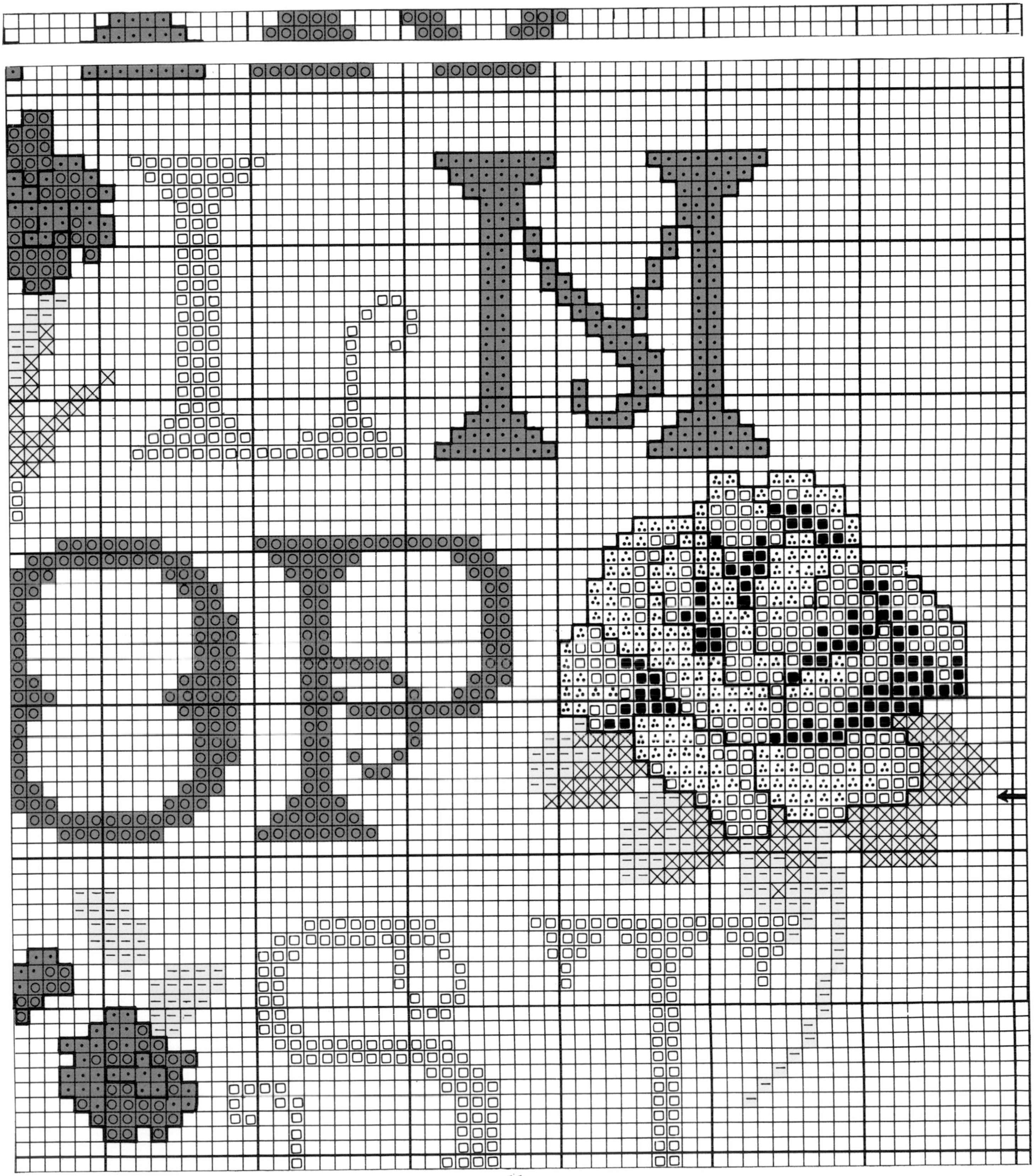

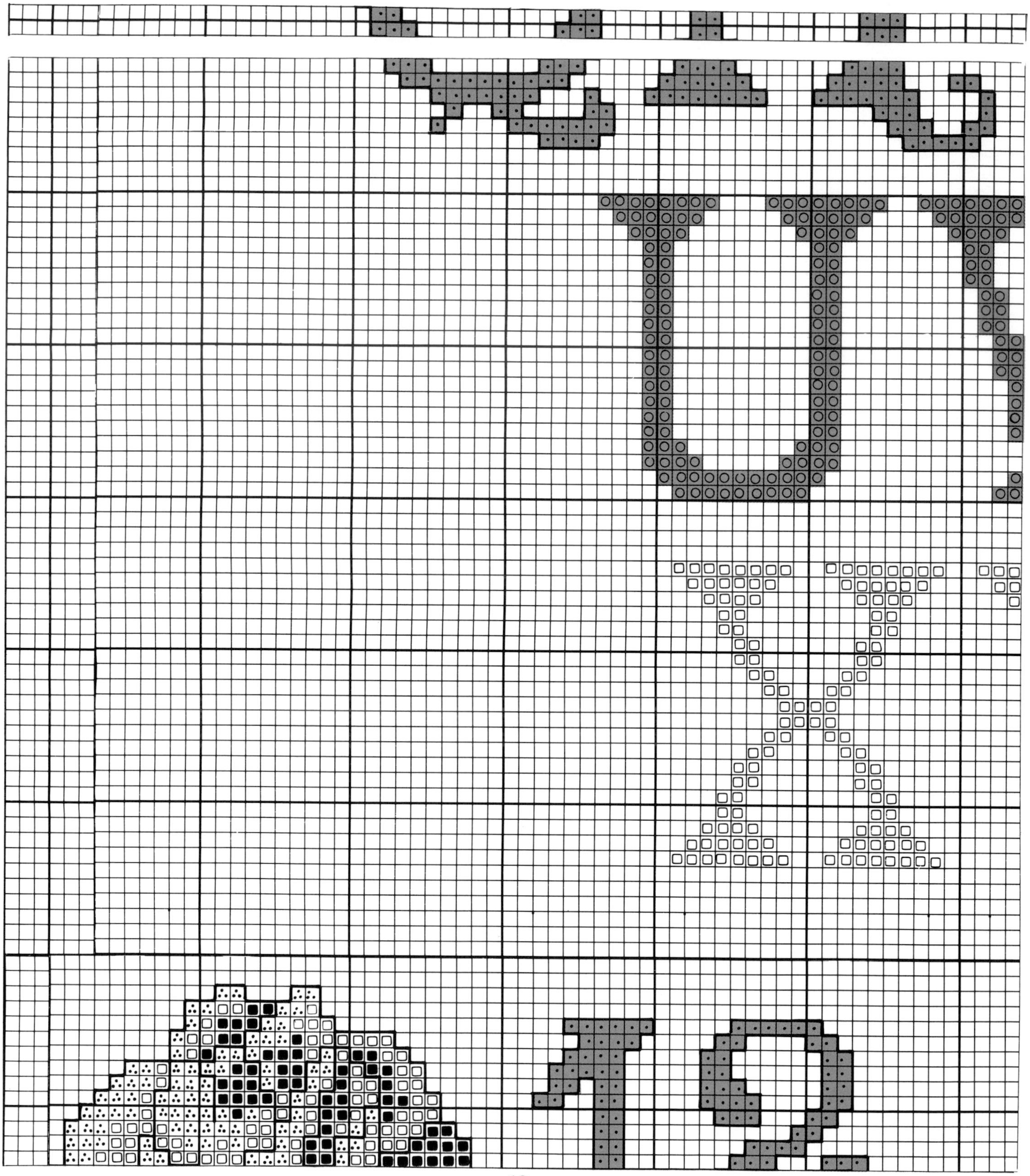

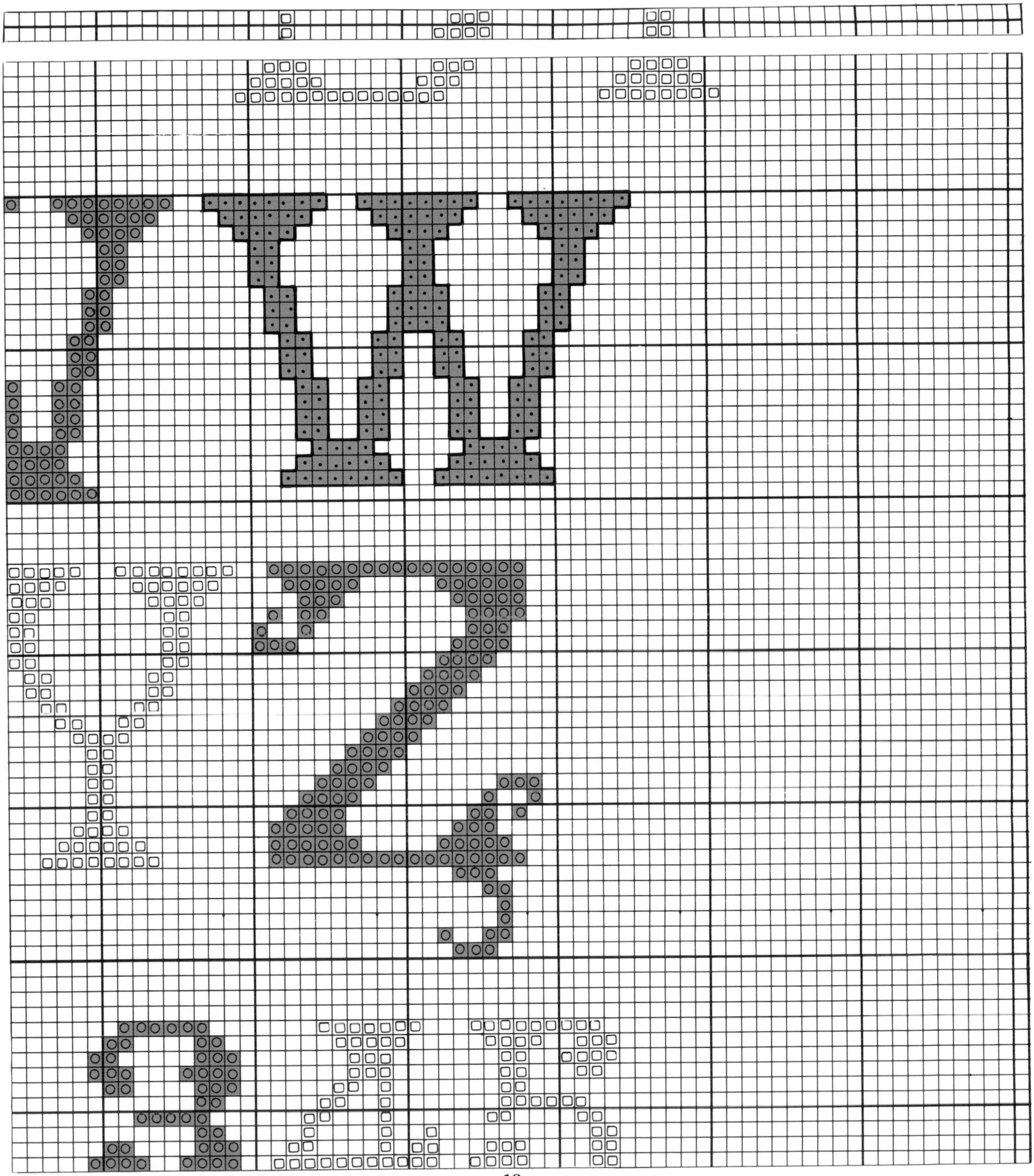

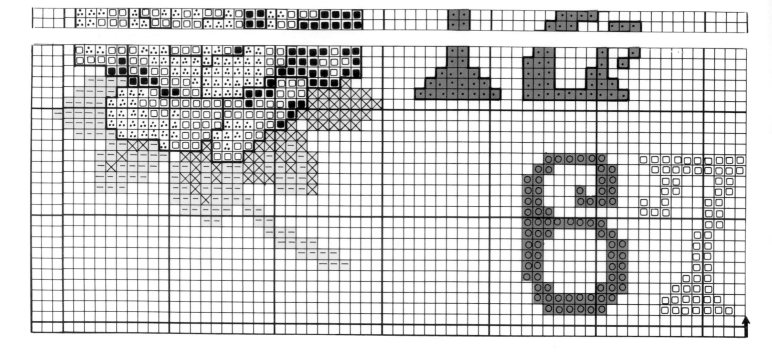

Garden of Letters

Alphabet: Stitched on Silk Gauze 30 over two threads, the finished design size is 8⅝" x 16⅜". The fabric was cut 16" x 26". To create three-dimensional effect when framing, align alphabet over flowers, inserting ¼"-thick spacers between foreground and background designs. See Suppliers for fabric.

FABRICS	DESIGN SIZES
Aida 11	11⅞" x 22¼"
Aida 14	9¼" x 17½"
Aida 18	7¼" x 13⅝"
Hardanger 22	5⅞" x 11⅛"

Flowers: The motif is from "Garden of Letters" (pages 16–17). See code on page 24. Stitched on amaretto Murano 30 over two threads, the finished design size is 4⅝" x 4⅜" for each repeat; stitch seven. Heavy black lines indicate repeats. Beginning in center of fabric, stitch Repeat A first. Begin bottom stitch of B, 35 stitches (70 threads) above top stitch of A. Begin top stitch of E, 35 stitches (70 threads) below bottom stitch of A. See Diagram 1 for placement. The fabric was cut 16" x 26".

FABRICS	DESIGN SIZES
Aida 11	6⅜" x 5⅞"
Aida 14	5" x 4⅝"
Aida 18	3⅞" x 3⅝"
Hardanger 22	3⅛" x 3"

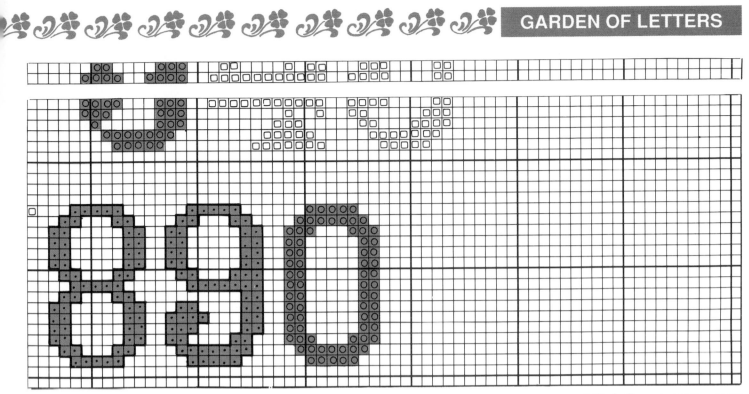

Stitch Count: 130 x 245

Anchor		DMC (used for sample)

Step 1: Cross-stitch (2 strands)

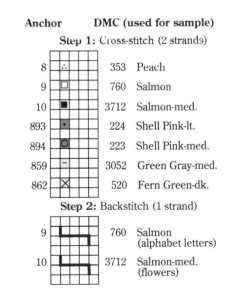

8	353	Peach
9	760	Salmon
10	3712	Salmon-med.
893	224	Shell Pink-lt.
894	223	Shell Pink-med.
859	3052	Green Gray-med.
862	520	Fern Green-dk.

Step 2: Backstitch (1 strand)

| 9 | 760 | Salmon (alphabet letters) |
| 10 | 3712 | Salmon-med. (flowers) |

Diagram 1

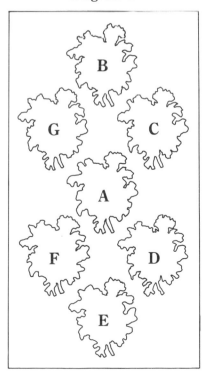

15

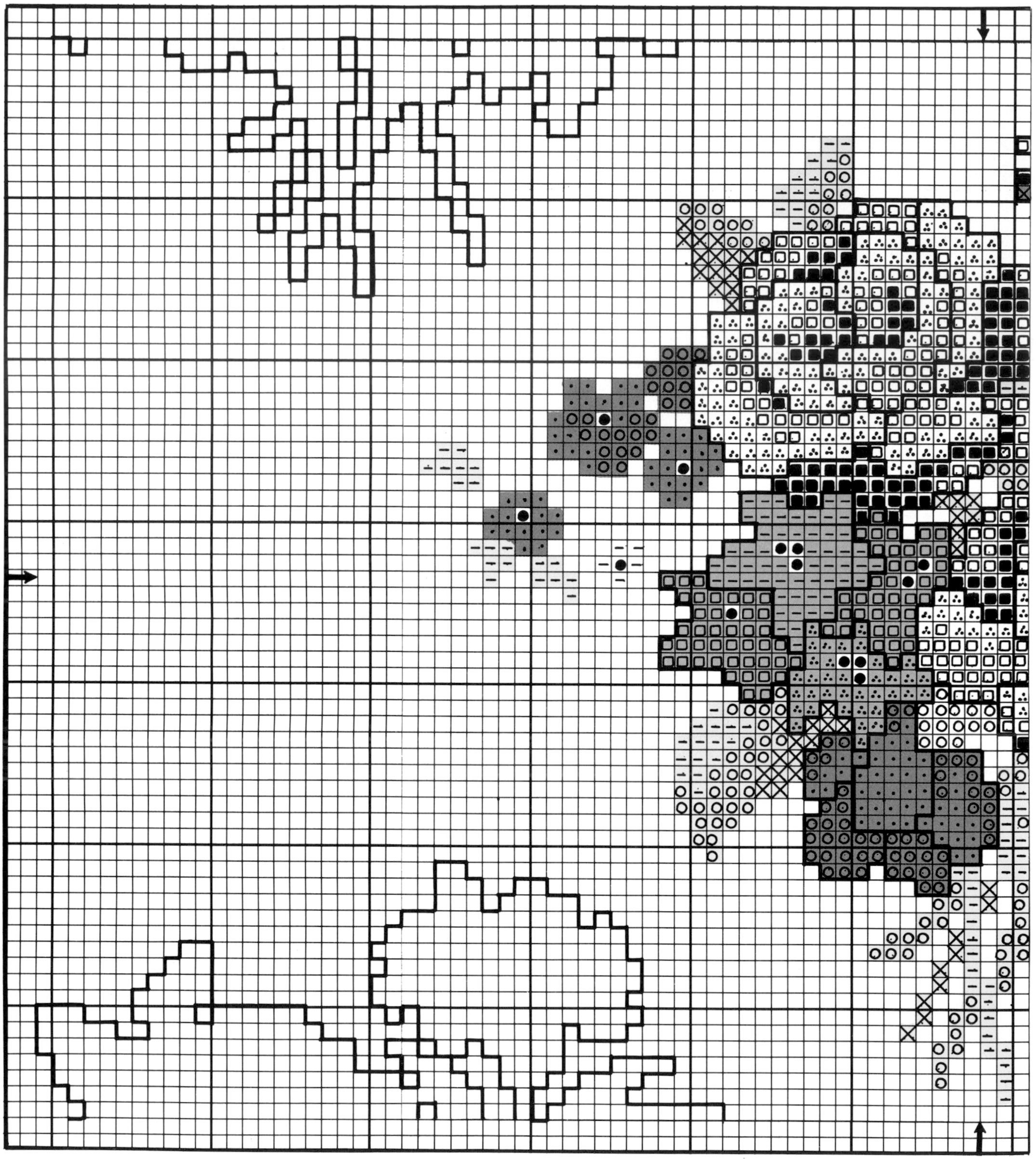

Stitch Count: 70 x 65 (for one repeat)

Precious Rose

The motif is from "Garden of Letters" (pages 8–17). Stitched on cream Belfast Linen 32 over two threads, the finished design size is 2" x 1⅞". The fabric was cut 8" x 8". Insert design piece in jar lid, following manufacturer's instructions. See Suppliers for jar.

FABRICS	DESIGN SIZES
Aida 11	2⅞" x 2¾"
Aida 14	2¼" x 2⅛"
Aida 18	1¾" x 1⅝"
Hardanger 22	1⅜" x 1⅜"

Clever Hideaway

Monogram: Stitched on Silk Gauze 30 over two threads, the finished design size varies with letters stitched. The fabric was cut 13" x 9". To personalize box, transfer desired letters to graph paper, spacing adequately between them. Mark centers of graph and begin stitching in center of space indicated. See Suppliers for fabric.

Flowers: Stitched on amaretto Murano 30 over two threads, the finished design size is 6⅛" x 2⅜". The fabric was cut 13" x 9". See graph below.

FABRICS	DESIGN SIZES
Aida 11	8⅜" x 3⅛"
Aida 14	6⅝" x 2½"
Aida 18	5⅛" x 2"
Hardanger 22	4⅛" x 1⅝"

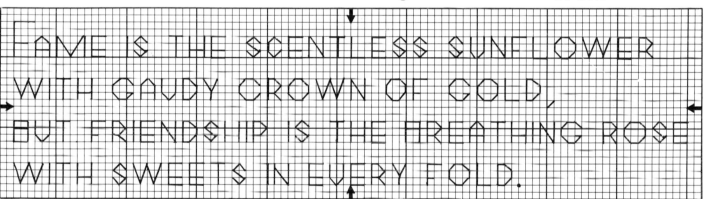

Stitch Count: 96 x 24

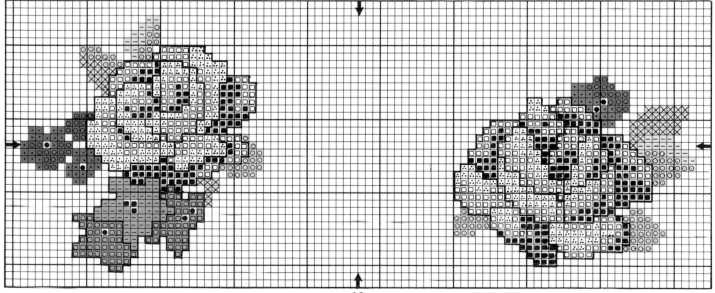

Stitch Count: 92 x 35

Saying: Stitched on amaretto Murano 30 over two threads, the finished design size is 6⅜" x 1⅝". The fabric was cut 13" x 9".

FABRICS
Aida 11
Aida 14
Aida 18
Hardanger 22

DESIGN SIZES
8¾" x 2⅛"
6⅞" x 1¾"
5⅜" x 1⅜"
4⅜" x 1⅛"

MATERIALS

Completed design piece on Silk Gauze 30
Two completed design pieces on amaretto Murano 30;
   matching thread
Wooden box*
Acrylic paints   Varnish
Paintbrushes   Fleece
Sponges   Mat board
Stencils   Glue gun and glue
White pencil   *see Suppliers

DIRECTIONS

1. Paint and stencil box as desired. Allow to dry. To create marbled effect, use white pencil to draw lines on box. Apply a thin coat of varnish. Allow to dry.

2. To complete model, zigzag around outer edges of each design piece. Cut three fleece pieces and one mat board piece to match insert. Also from mat board scraps, cut four spacers.

3. For outside of lid, glue one fleece piece to insert. Center flowers over fleece; fold excess fabric to back and glue to insert. To create three-dimensional effect, insert spacers between background and foreground designs. Then center monogram over flowers; fold to back and glue to insert. Place in lid with right side out.

4. For inside of lid, center and glue remaining fleece pieces and saying to mat board insert. Place in lid, gluing backs of inserts together so that saying is right side up when lid is opened.

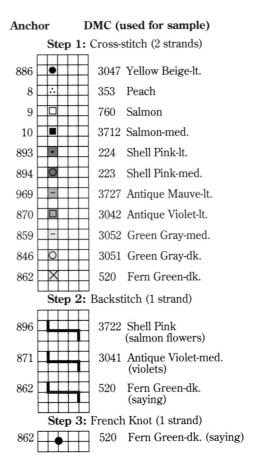

Anchor		DMC (used for sample)	
Step 1: Cross-stitch (2 strands)			
886	●	3047	Yellow Beige-lt.
8	∴	353	Peach
9	□	760	Salmon
10	■	3712	Salmon-med.
893	·	224	Shell Pink-lt.
894	○	223	Shell Pink-med.
969	−	3727	Antique Mauve-lt.
870	□	3042	Antique Violet-lt.
859	−	3052	Green Gray-med.
846	○	3051	Green Gray-dk.
862	✕	520	Fern Green-dk.
Step 2: Backstitch (1 strand)			
896		3722	Shell Pink (salmon flowers)
871		3041	Antique Violet-med. (violets)
862		520	Fern Green-dk. (saying)
Step 3: French Knot (1 strand)			
862	●	520	Fern Green-dk. (saying)

Fame is the scentless sunflower
With gaudy crown of gold,
But friendship is the breathing rose
With sweets in every fold.

Luminous Roses

The motif is from "Rose Tray" (pages 23–24). Stitched on white Belfast Linen 32 over two threads, the finished design size is 4¼" x 4". Disregard heavy black lines that indicate repeats. The fabric was cut 28" x 16".

FABRICS	DESIGN SIZES
Aida 11	6¼" x 5⅞"
Aida 14	4⅞" x 4⅝"
Aida 18	3⅞" x 3⅝"
Hardanger 22	3⅛" x 3"

MATERIALS

Completed design piece on white Belfast Linen 32; matching thread
⅜ yard of white cotton for lining
1¼ yards of 2"-wide gathered rust netting
21½" x 9¼" tube style lamp shade
Glue
Dressmaker's pen

DIRECTIONS

All seams are ¼".

1. Cut design piece and lining to 22" x 10". Cut netting into two equal lengths.

2. With right sides facing and raw edges aligned, stitch 10" edges of design piece, forming a tube. Turn. Repeat for lining.

3. With right sides facing and raw edges aligned, stitch bottom edge of design piece to lining. Turn. Slide over lamp shade with lining to inside and stitched seam at bottom.

4. For strut opening, clip from lining top edge to just below strut. Turn under raw edges and smooth lining around strut. Slipstitch opening closed. Repeat.

5. Turn under seam allowance and slipstitch top of lining and design piece together.

6. On outside of lamp shade, mark 1" from top edge and glue one netting length in place, starting and ending at back seam. Repeat on bottom edge for remaining netting length.

Rose Tray

Stitched on amaretto Murano 30 over two threads, the finished design size is 4⅝" x 4⅜" for each repeat; stitch two. Heavy black lines indicate repeats. The fabric was cut 16" x 11".

FABRICS	DESIGN SIZES
Aida 11	6⅜" x 5⅞"
Aida 14	5" x 4⅝"
Aida 18	3⅞" x 3⅝"
Hardanger 22	3⅛" x 3"

MATERIALS

Completed design piece on amaretto Murano 30
Mat board
Tray
Glue

DIRECTIONS

1. Measure tray insert. Cut mat board to match. To complete model, zigzag outer edges of design piece. Center over mat board, folding excess to back; glue. Insert into tray.

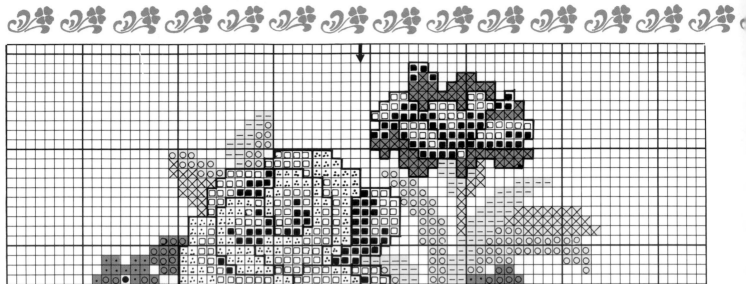

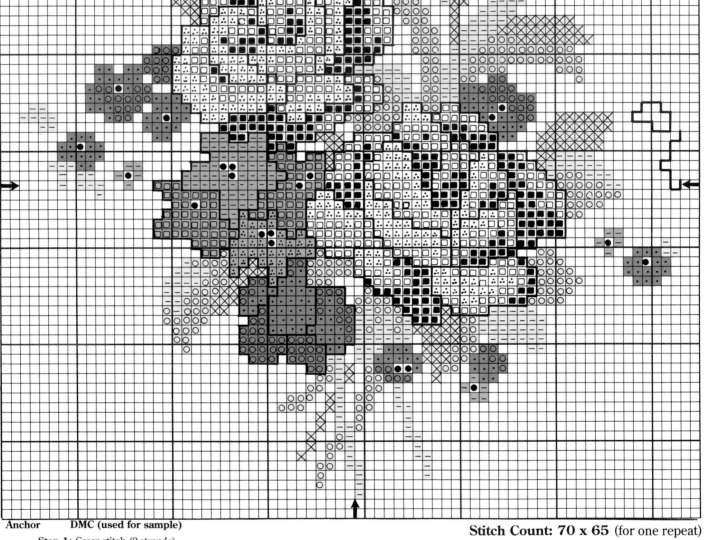

Anchor   DMC (used for sample)

Stitch Count: 70 x 65 (for one repeat)

Step 1: Cross-stitch (2 strands)

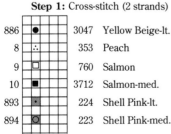

886	●	3047	Yellow Beige-lt.
8	∴	353	Peach
9	□	760	Salmon
10	■	3712	Salmon-med.
893	·	224	Shell Pink-lt.
894	◎	223	Shell Pink-med.

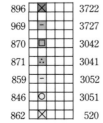

896	⊠	3722	Shell Pink
969	–	3727	Antique Mauve-lt.
870	▢	3042	Antique Violet-lt.
871	∴	3041	Antique Violet-med.
859	–	3052	Green Gray-med.
846	○	3051	Green Gray-dk.
862	⨯	520	Fern Green-dk.

Step 2: Backstitch (1 strand)

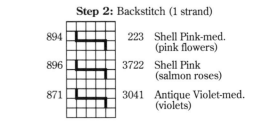

894		223	Shell Pink-med. (pink flowers)
896		3722	Shell Pink (salmon roses)
871		3041	Antique Violet-med. (violets)

24

On a warm summer day, a child visits a favorite shady spot in the garden. Friendly bluebirds and magic flower garlands fly the young adventurer across the clear skies. They arrive home in time to pick a basketful of daisies before lunch. Even when childhood ends, the delightful memory of summer daydreams remains.

30

31

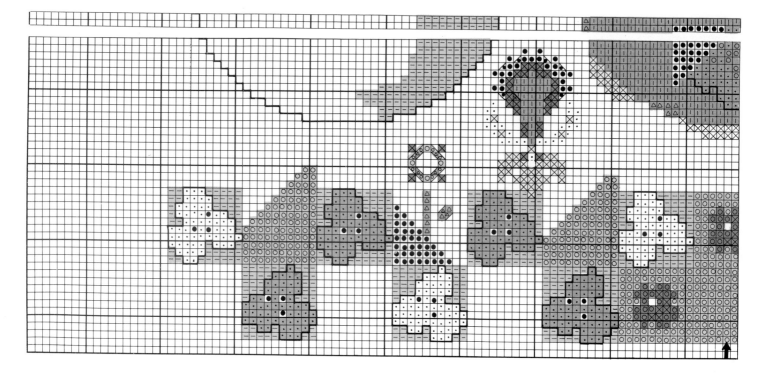

You Lift Me Up

Stitched on cream Murano 30 over two threads, the finished design size is 12¼" x 16½". The fabric was cut 19" x 23".

FABRICS	DESIGN SIZES
Aida 11	16⅝" x 22½"
Aida 14	13⅛" x 17¾"
Aida 18	10⅛" x 13¾"
Hardanger 22	8⅜" x 11¼"

Anchor   **DMC (used for sample)**

Step 1: Cross-stitch (2 strands)

886			677	Old Gold-vy. lt.
881			3779	Terra Cotta-vy. lt.
868			758	Terra Cotta-lt.
5975			356	Terra Cotta-med.
349			921	Copper
339			920	Copper-med.
892			225	Shell Pink-vy. lt.
894			223	Shell Pink-med.
896			3722	Shell Pink
869			3743	Antique Violet-vy. lt.
110			208	Lavender-vy. dk.
158			828	Blue-ultra vy. lt.
121			793	Cornflower Blue-med.
816			3750	Antique Blue-vy. dk.
849			927	Slate Green-med.
840			3768	Slate Green-dk.
875			503	Blue Green-med.
876			502	Blue Green
862			3362	Pine Green-dk.
903			640	Beige Gray-vy. dk.
8581			646	Beaver Gray-dk.

Step 2: Backstitch (1 strand)

158		828	Blue-ultra vy. lt. (blue circle outlines)
236		3799	Pewter Gray-vy. dk. (all else)

Framed Fancy

Stitch Count: 183 x 248

Girl: The motif is from "You Lift Me Up" (pages 28–33). Stitched on cream Murano 30 over two threads, the finished design size is 6⅝" x 6⅞". The fabric was cut 13" x 13".

FABRICS	DESIGN SIZES
Aida 11	9" x 9⅜"
Aida 14	7⅛" x 7⅜"
Aida 18	5½" x 5¾"
Hardanger 22	4½" x 4⅝"

Basket: The motif is from "You Lift Me Up" (pages 28–33). Stitched on cream Murano 30 over two threads, the finished design size is 2⅛" x 2⅛". The fabric was cut 9" x 9". Cut and stitch four.

FABRICS	DESIGN SIZES
Aida 11	3" x 2⅞"
Aida 14	2¼" x 2¼"
Aida 18	1¾" x 1¾"
Hardanger 22	1½" x 1⅜"

Rose: The motif is from "You Lift Me Up" (pages 28–33). Stitched on cream Murano 30, the finished design size is 2¾" x 2¾". The fabric was cut 9" x 9". Cut and stitch four.

FABRICS	DESIGN SIZES
Aida 11	3⅝" x 3⅝"
Aida 14	2⅞" x 2⅞"
Aida 18	2¼" x 2¼"
Hardanger 22	1⅛" x 1⅞"

MATERIALS

Completed 13" x 13" design piece on cream Murano 30
Eight completed 9" x 9" design pieces on cream Murano 30
Novelty frame with eight 3" round windows surrounding one 7" round window
Mat board
Scraps of fleece
Glue

DIRECTIONS

1. Make one 8" and one 4" circle pattern. Center 8" circle pattern over 13" x 13" design piece; cut. Center 4" circle pattern over one 9" x 9" design piece; cut. Repeat for remaining 9"x 9" design pieces.

2. Cut one 7" circle and eight 3" circles from mat board and from fleece.

33

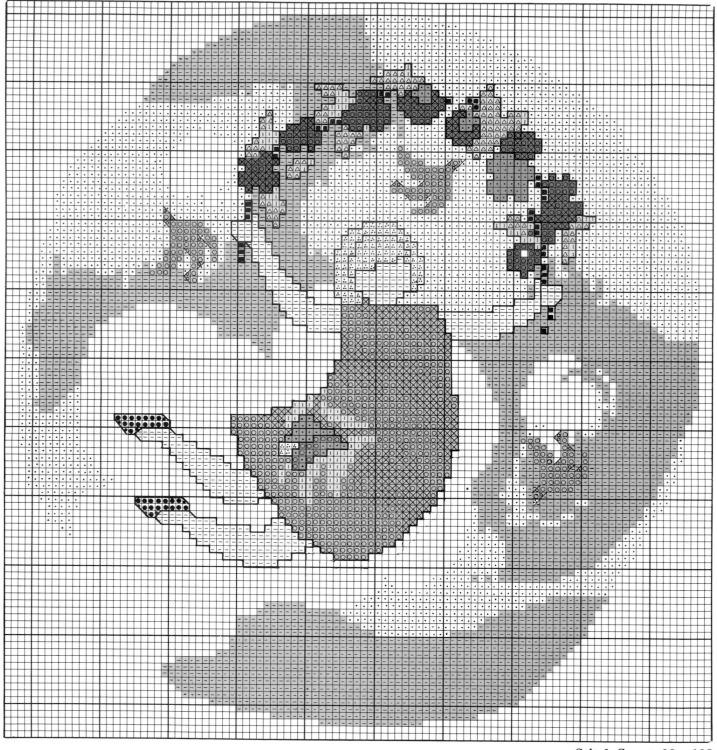

Stitch Count: 99 x 103

3. Glue fleece to mat board. Center large design on fleece-covered side of mat board. Fold excess fabric to back and glue. Repeat with smaller design pieces and mat board circles.

4. Insert design pieces into windows, securing with frame back.

Keeping Secrets

Pink Flowers: Stitched on cream Belfast Linen 32 over two threads, the finished design size 5⅞" x 5½". The fabric was cut 9" x 9".

Peach Flowers: Stitched on driftwood Belfast Linen 32 over two threads, the finished design size 5⅞" x 5½". The fabric was cut 9" x 9".

For both, begin stitching corner of design 1¼" from each edge of lower right corner of fabric. Extend border 6½" each direction.

FABRICS	DESIGN SIZES
Aida 11	8½" x 8"
Aida 14	6¾" x 6¼"
Aida 18	5¼" x 4⅞"
Hardanger 22	4¼" x 4"

Anchor   **DMC (used for sample)**

Step 1: Cross-stitch (2 strands)

Anchor		DMC	
868	■	758	Terra Cotta-lt.
66	◉	3688	Mauve med.
69	✕	3687	Mauve
870	–	3042	Antique Violet-lt.
343	✕	3752	Antique Blue-ultra vy. lt.
876	○	502	Blue Green
878	✕	501	Blue Green-dk.
942	△	738	Tan-vy. lt.

Step 2: Backstitch (1 strand)

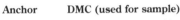

382		3021	Brown Gray-vy. dk.

Anchor   **DMC (used for sample)**

Step 1: Cross-stitch (2 strands)

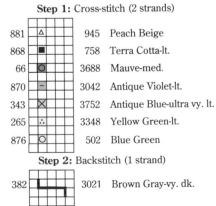

Anchor		DMC	
881	△	945	Peach Beige
868	■	758	Terra Cotta-lt.
66	◉	3688	Mauve-med.
870	–	3042	Antique Violet-lt.
343	✕	3752	Antique Blue-ultra vy. lt.
265	∴	3348	Yellow Green-lt.
876	○	502	Blue Green

Step 2: Backstitch (1 strand)

382		3021	Brown Gray-vy. dk.

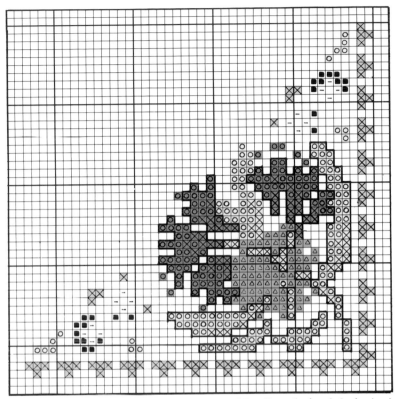

Stitch Count: 94 x 88 (for whole pink design)

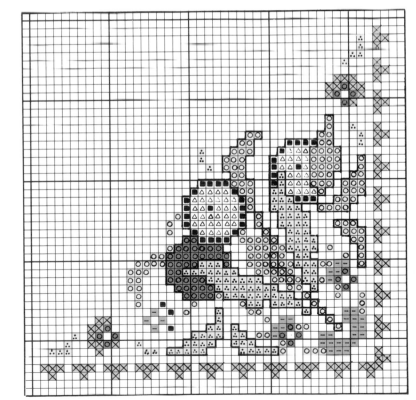

Stitch Count: 94 x 88 (for whole peach design)

MATERIALS (for one)

Completed design piece on cream or driftwood Belfast
    Linen 32; matching thread
⅜ yard of unstitched cream or driftwood Belfast Linen 32
⅜ yard of lining fabric
1½ yards of ½"-wide cream satin trim

DIRECTIONS

1. Enlarge and make triangle pattern. Place pattern over
design piece with sides of 90° angle parallel to and 1" from
outside edges of design piece. Cut one envelope flap.
From unstitched linen, cut one 10" x 10" piece and four
additional triangles. From lining fabric, cut one triangle
and two 10" x 10" pieces.

2. To make envelope front, use a ½" seam to stitch
together two unstitched linen triangle pieces. Repeat with
remaining unstitched linen triangle pieces. Open. With
right sides facing and long edges aligned, join two triangle
pairs to form square; see Diagram 1. Press seams open.
Topstitch on both sides of each seam, stitching ⅛" from
and parallel to seam through all layers.

3. Stitch envelope front to back on three sides. Clip
corners. Turn. Stitch design piece to lining triangle on
two short sides. Clip corners. Turn.

4. Cut one 15" length of trim. Slipstitch to short edges of
design piece on right side.

5. Match long edge of design piece to top edge of envelope back with right sides facing. Stitch from seam
allowance to seam allowance through all layers;
backstitch.

6. Stitch lining front to back; do not turn. Stitch lining over
envelope with design flap between lining and back. Stitch
around top edge, leaving an opening. Clip corners. Turn.
Fold lining inside envelope. Slipstitch opening closed.

7. Slipstitch trim to right side of envelope front on all
edges.

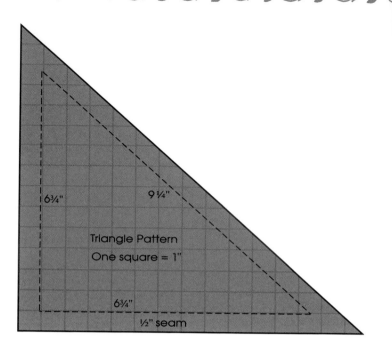

6¾"   9¼"

Triangle Pattern
One square = 1"

6¾"

½" seam

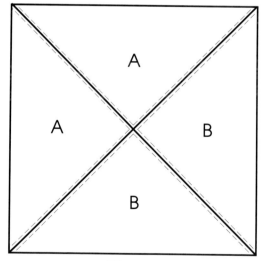

A

A   B

B

Diagram 1

Jewelry Keeper

The motif is from "You Lift Me Up" (pages 28–33). Stitched on cream Murano 30 over two threads, the finished design is 3⅝" x 3⅝". The fabric was cut 10" x 10". Insert design piece in jar lid, following manufacturer's instructions. See Suppliers for jar.

FABRICS
Aida 11
Aida 14
Aida 18
Hardanger 22

DESIGN SIZES
4⅞" x 4⅞"
3⅞" x 3⅞"
3" x 3"
2½" x 2½"

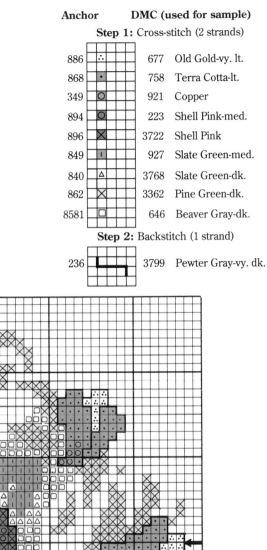

Anchor		DMC (used for sample)	
Step 1: Cross-stitch (2 strands)			
886		677	Old Gold-vy. lt.
868		758	Terra Cotta-lt.
349		921	Copper
894		223	Shell Pink-med.
896		3722	Shell Pink
849		927	Slate Green-med.
840		3768	Slate Green-dk.
862		3362	Pine Green-dk.
8581		646	Beaver Gray-dk.
Step 2: Backstitch (1 strand)			
236		3799	Pewter Gray-vy. dk.

Stitch Count: 54 x 54

Butterfly Wings

Stitched on ash rose Murano 30 over two threads, the finished design size is 2⅛" x 1⅞" for each repeat; stitch nine. The fabric was cut 6" x 26". Heavy black lines indicate repeats.

FABRICS	DESIGN SIZES
Aida 11	2⅞" x 2⅝"
Aida 14	2¼" x 2⅛"
Aida 18	1¾" x 1⅝"
Hardanger 22	1⅜" x 1⅜"

MATERIALS

Completed design piece on ash rose Murano 30; matching thread
One 2¾" x 20" piece of unstitched ash rose Murano 30 for back
1¼ yards of floral print polished cotton
1¼ yards of mauve polished cotton fabric; matching thread
5 yards of ¼"-wide cording
1¼ yards of fleece
Polyester stuffing

DIRECTIONS

All seams are ¼".

1. With design centered, cut design piece to measure 2¾" x 20". From fleece, cut one 2¾" x 20" strip. Cut two 20" x 13" pieces each of print fabric and fleece. Also from print fabric, cut 1"-wide bias strips, piecing as needed to equal 3 yards. Make corded piping. Cut two 18" x 9" pieces each of mauve fabric and fleece. Also from mauve fabric, cut 1"-wide bias strips, piecing as needed to equal 2 yards. Make corded piping.

2. Zigzag 2¾" fleece strip to wrong side of design piece. Press if needed. With right sides facing and raw edges aligned, stitch a 20" length of print piping on each long edge of design piece. Repeat to stitch design piece to back, following stitching line of piping. Turn. Set aside.

3. For print pillow, zigzag fleece to wrong side of pillow front and back. Press if needed. With right sides facing and raw edges aligned, stitch mauve piping to pillow front edges, rounding corners slightly. Stitch pillow front to back on stitching line of piping, leaving an opening. Turn. Stuff moderately. Slipstitch opening closed.

4. Repeat Step 3 to make mauve pillow with remaining print piping.

5. Position mauve pillow on top of print pillow. Wrap design piece around middle of pillows, easing fullness; see photo. Turn under seam allowance on one end of design piece. Insert remaining raw end and slipstitch securely.

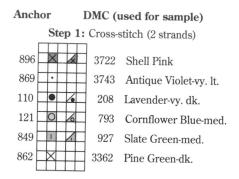

Anchor		DMC (used for sample)	
	Step 1:	Cross-stitch (2 strands)	
896		3722	Shell Pink
869		3743	Antique Violet-vy. lt.
110		208	Lavender-vy. dk.
121		793	Cornflower Blue-med.
849		927	Slate Green-med.
862		3362	Pine Green-dk.

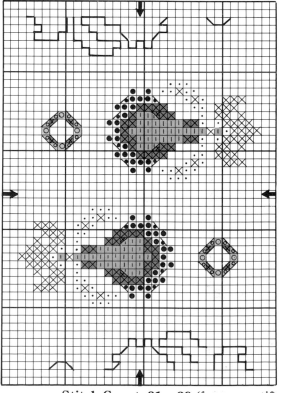

Stitch Count: 31 x 29 (for one motif)

In a Southern garden, a mother teaches the gentle art of decorating with fresh flowers. The mingled scents and delicate colors furnish the home place with grace and serenity.

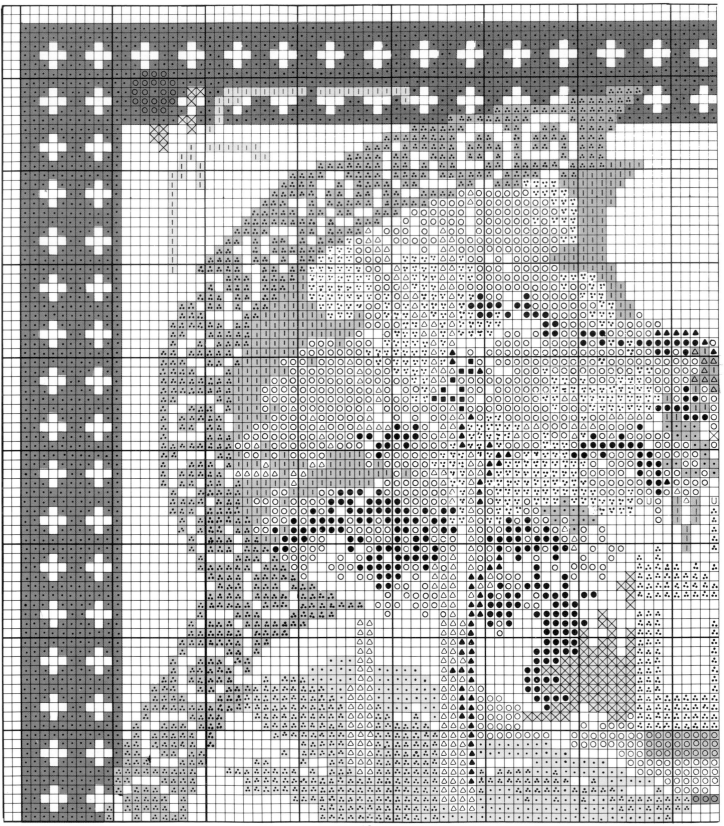

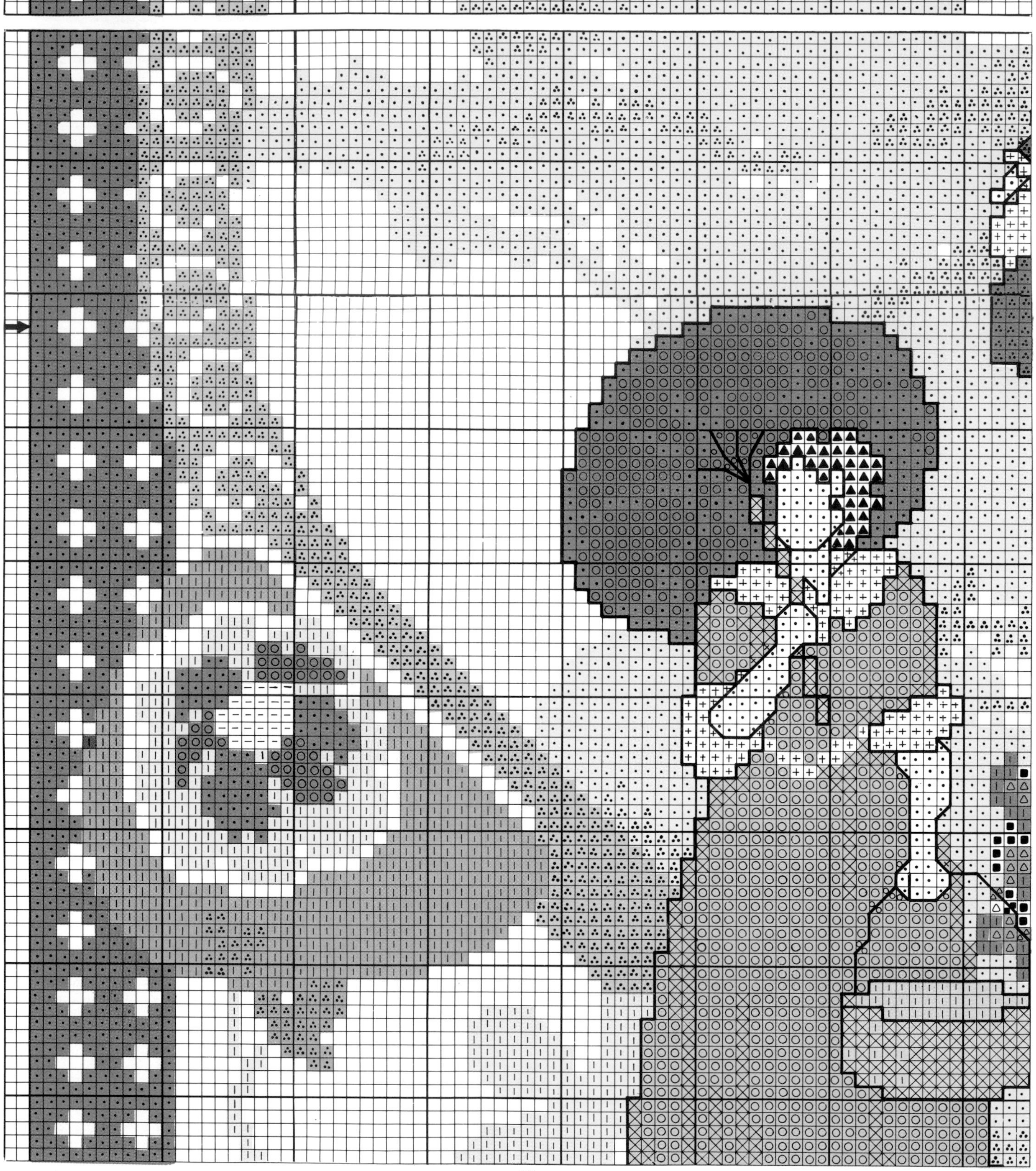

49

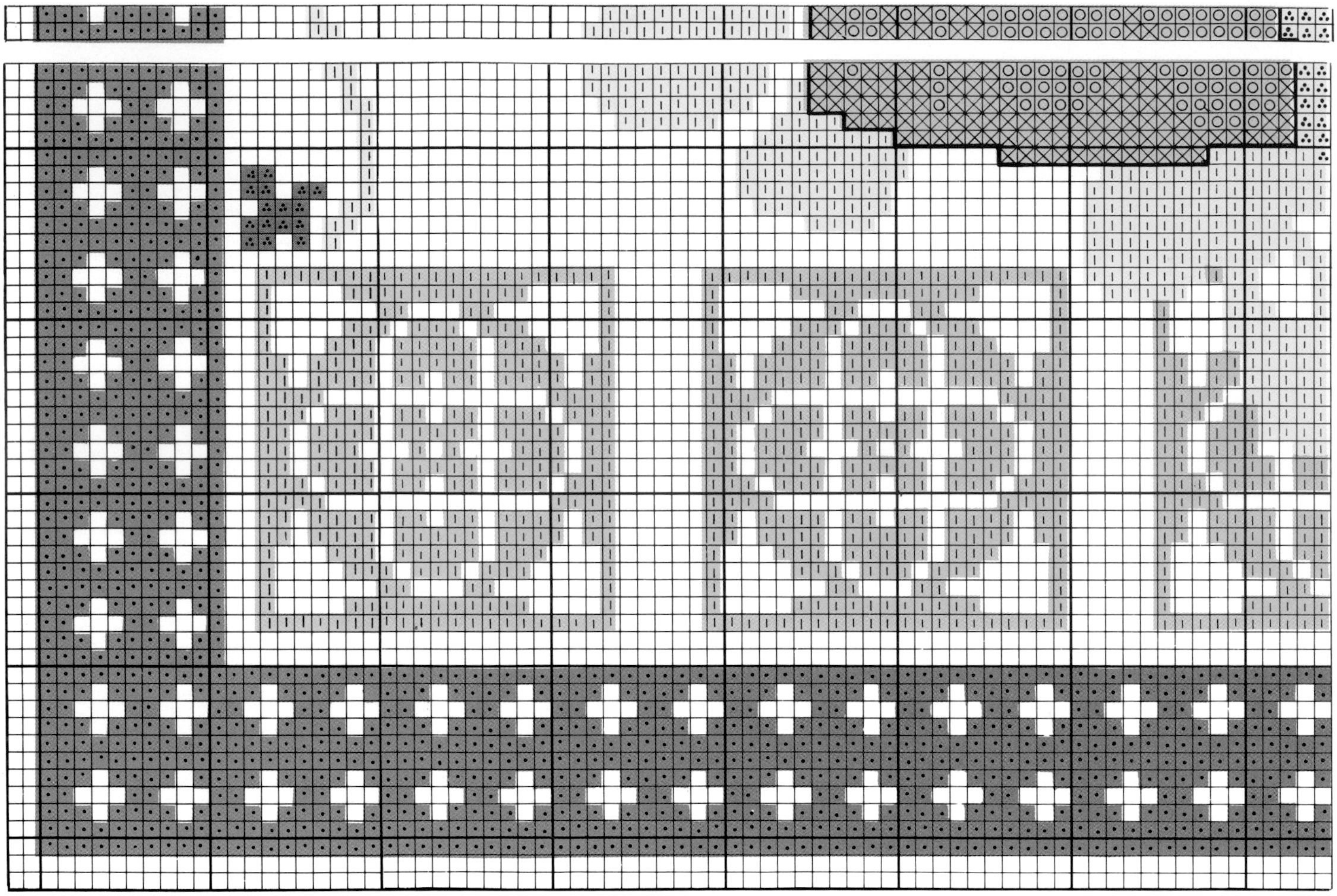

Stitch Count: 151 x 217

Magnolia Ladies

Stitched on white Dublin Linen 25 over two threads, the finished design size is 12⅛" x 17⅜". The fabric was cut 19" x 24".

FABRICS	DESIGN SIZES
Aida 11	13¾" x 19¾"
Aida 14	10¾" x 15½"
Aida 18	8⅜" x 12"
Hardanger 22	6⅞" x 9⅞"

Anchor		DMC	(used for sample)

Step 1: Cross-stitch (2 strands)

Anchor		DMC	
1	+ /		White
300	−	745	Yellow-lt. pale
886	X	677	Old Gold-vy. lt.
778	· /	948	Peach-vy. lt.
868	∴	758	Terra Cotta-lt.
5975	U	356	Terra Cotta-med.
892	O	225	Shell Pink-vy. lt.
893	·	224	Shell Pink-lt.
50	I	605	Cranberry-vy. lt.
42	∴ /	3350	Dusty Rose-dk.
43	X	815	Garnet-med.
95	∴	554	Violet-lt.
869	I	3743	Antique Violet-vy. lt.

Anchor		DMC	
872	△	3740	Antique Violet-dk.
975	·	3756	Baby Blue-ultra vy. lt.
158	I /	828	Blue-ultra vy. lt.
159	△	827	Blue-vy. lt.
920	∴	932	Antique Blue-lt. (1 strand)
978	O /	322	Navy Blue-vy. lt.
149	X /	311	Navy Blue-med.
840	□	3768	Slate Green-dk.
212	■	561	Jade-vy. dk.
875	I	503	Blue Green-med.
878	X	501	Blue Green-dk.
215	· /	320	Pistachio Green-med.
246	∴ /	319	Pistachio Green-vy. dk.
859	O	522	Fern Green
862	●	520	Fern Green-dk.
956	∴	613	Drab Brown-lt.
379	△	840	Beige Brown-med.
380	▲ /	839	Beige Brown-dk.
914	I	3772	Pecan-med.
349	O	301	Mahogany-med.
352	X /	300	Mahogany-vy. dk.
397	O	453	Shell Gray-lt.
399	X	452	Shell Gray-med.

Step 2: Backstitch (1 strand)

Anchor		DMC	
236	⌐	3799	Pewter Gray-vy. dk.

Pocket Full O' Flowers

Stitched on light blue Jobelan 28 over two threads, the finished design size is 5" x 6⅜". The fabric was cut 9" x 11". More than one thread color represented by a single symbol on the code and graph indicates blending; note number of strands used. See Suppliers for fabric.

FABRICS	DESIGN SIZES
Aida 11	6⅜" x 8⅛"
Aida 14	5" x 6⅜"
Aida 18	3⅞" x 5"
Hardanger 22	3⅛" x 4⅛"

MATERIALS

Completed design piece on light blue Jobelan 28;
   matching thread
¼ yard of light mauve fabric; matching thread
Adult's cotton shirt
Dressmaker's pen

DIRECTIONS

1. Cut design piece to 5" x 6¾" with design centered. From mauve fabric, cut one 5" x 6¾" lining piece and ⅞"-wide bias, piecing as needed to equal ⅝ yard. Cut bias into one 5" and one 17½" length.

2. Fold bias in half lengthwise and press. With right sides facing and raw edges aligned, baste 5" bias length to top edge of design piece. Bias will extend above design piece about ⅛". Baste 17½" length around design piece, slightly rounding corners and allowing ends to extend ¼" above each top corner. With right sides facing and raw edges aligned, stitch lining to design piece, leaving top edges unstitched. Clip corners. Turn. Fold top edge of lining and bias ends to inside. Slipstitch.

3. Mark pocket placement on shirt. Pin pocket to shirt. With mauve thread, topstitch pocket to shirt in the ditch on the bias, leaving the top open.

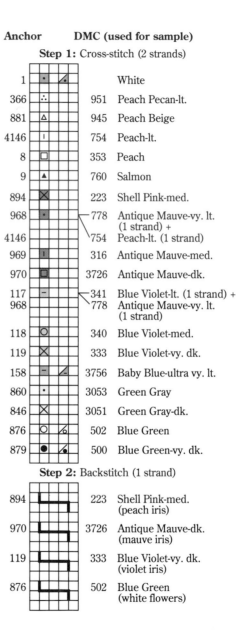

Anchor		DMC (used for sample)
Step 1: Cross-stitch (2 strands)		
1		White
366		951 Peach Pecan-lt.
881		945 Peach Beige
4146		754 Peach-lt.
8		353 Peach
9		760 Salmon
894		223 Shell Pink-med.
968		778 Antique Mauve-vy. lt. (1 strand) +
4146		754 Peach-lt. (1 strand)
969		316 Antique Mauve-med.
970		3726 Antique Mauve-dk.
117		341 Blue Violet-lt. (1 strand) +
968		778 Antique Mauve-vy. lt. (1 strand)
118		340 Blue Violet-med.
119		333 Blue Violet-vy. dk.
158		3756 Baby Blue-ultra vy. lt.
860		3053 Green Gray
846		3051 Green Gray-dk.
876		502 Blue Green
879		500 Blue Green-vy. dk.
Step 2: Backstitch (1 strand)		
894		223 Shell Pink-med. (peach iris)
970		3726 Antique Mauve-dk. (mauve iris)
119		333 Blue Violet-vy. dk. (violet iris)
876		502 Blue Green (white flowers)

Stitch Count: 70 x 90

Little Lights

Stitched on white Belfast Linen 32 over two threads, the finished design size is 1¼" x 1¼" for each motif; stitch three vertical pairs, centering first pair. The fabric was cut 13" x 10". Heavy black lines indicate placement of repeats.

FABRICS	**DESIGN SIZES**
Aida 11	1⅞" x 1⅞"
Aida 14	1½" x 1½"
Aida 18	1⅛" x 1⅛"
Hardanger 22	1" x 1"

MATERIALS (for one)

Completed design piece on white Belfast Linen 32;
    matching thread
Glass candle holder with 6¾" x 3½" stem
Candle

DIRECTIONS

All seams are ¼".

1. With design centered, cut design piece to 7½" x 7".

2. With right sides facing and long edges aligned, stitch design piece, forming a tube and leaving ends open. Turn. Center seam to back and press.

3. Turn under seam allowance on one end of band. Wrap band around candle holder stem. Tuck in remaining end of band into folded end. Slipstitch ends together.

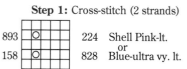

Anchor		DMC (used for sample)
	Step 1: Cross-stitch (2 strands)	
893		224 Shell Pink-lt.
158		828 Blue-ultra vy. lt.

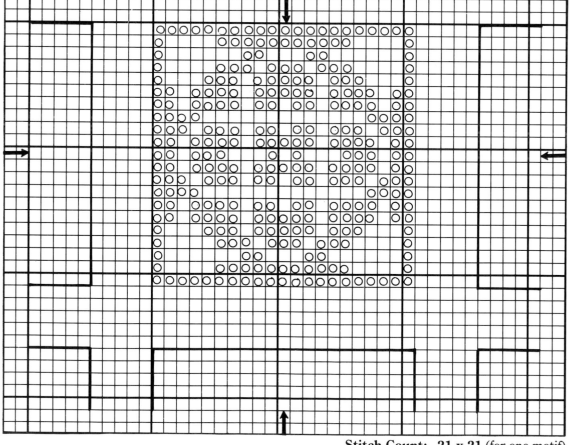

Stitch Count: 21 x 21 (for one motif)

Prissy Pillow

The motif is from "Magnolia Ladies" on (pages 46–52). Stitched on ice blue Annabelle 28 over two threads, the finished design size is 6⅜" x 5⅞". The fabric was cut 16" x 16".

FABRICS / DESIGN SIZES

FABRICS	DESIGN SIZES
Aida 11	8⅛" x 7½"
Aida 14	6⅜" x 5⅞"
Aida 18	5" x 4½"
Hardanger 22	4" x 3¾"

MATERIALS

Completed design piece on ice blue Annabelle 28; matching thread
One 11" x 11" piece of muslin
1 yard of print fabric; matching thread
4 yards of ⅛"-wide burgundy silk ribbon
Polyester stuffing
One small wooden bird
One ¾" mauve porcelain rose
Two ½" white porcelain roses
Seven ⅜" multi-colored porcelain roses
17 light yellow flat faceted beads
17 dark green flat faceted beads
1⅜ yards of silk French Rosette trim*; matching thread
Glue gun and glue
*see Suppliers

DIRECTIONS

All seams are ¼".

1. Cut design piece to 10½" x 9½" with design centered. Cut muslin to 10½" x 9½". For pillow back, cut one 10½" x 9½" piece from print fabric. Also from print fabric cut 6½"-wide bias strips, piecing as needed to equal 3⅛ yards for ruffle. Cut silk ribbon into ten equal lengths.

2. Zigzag muslin to wrong side of design piece.

3. Fold bias strip in half lengthwise and press. Sew gathering threads on long raw edge. Mark center of each design piece edge. Fold ruffle into quarters and mark. Match marks on ruffle to marks on design piece. Gather ruffle to fit; stitch to design piece with raw edges aligned. Stitch pillow front to back with right sides facing, leaving an opening. Clip corners. Turn.

4. Stuff pillow firmly. Slipstitch opening closed.

5. Slipstitch silk rose trim in gutter between ruffle and design piece; see photo. Glue bird, porcelain roses and beads to design piece as desired; see photo.

6. Handling five ribbon lengths as one, tie a bow. Repeat with remaining ribbon lengths. Glue one bow to top right hand corner of pillow front. Glue remaining bow directly over first.

*To a child, the
garden's lure is
irresistible in the
golden days of spring
and summer. Each
day yields new beau-
ties. Mother's flower
basket waits in the
dappled shade of the
trellis, filled with the
careful selections of
small, loving hands.*

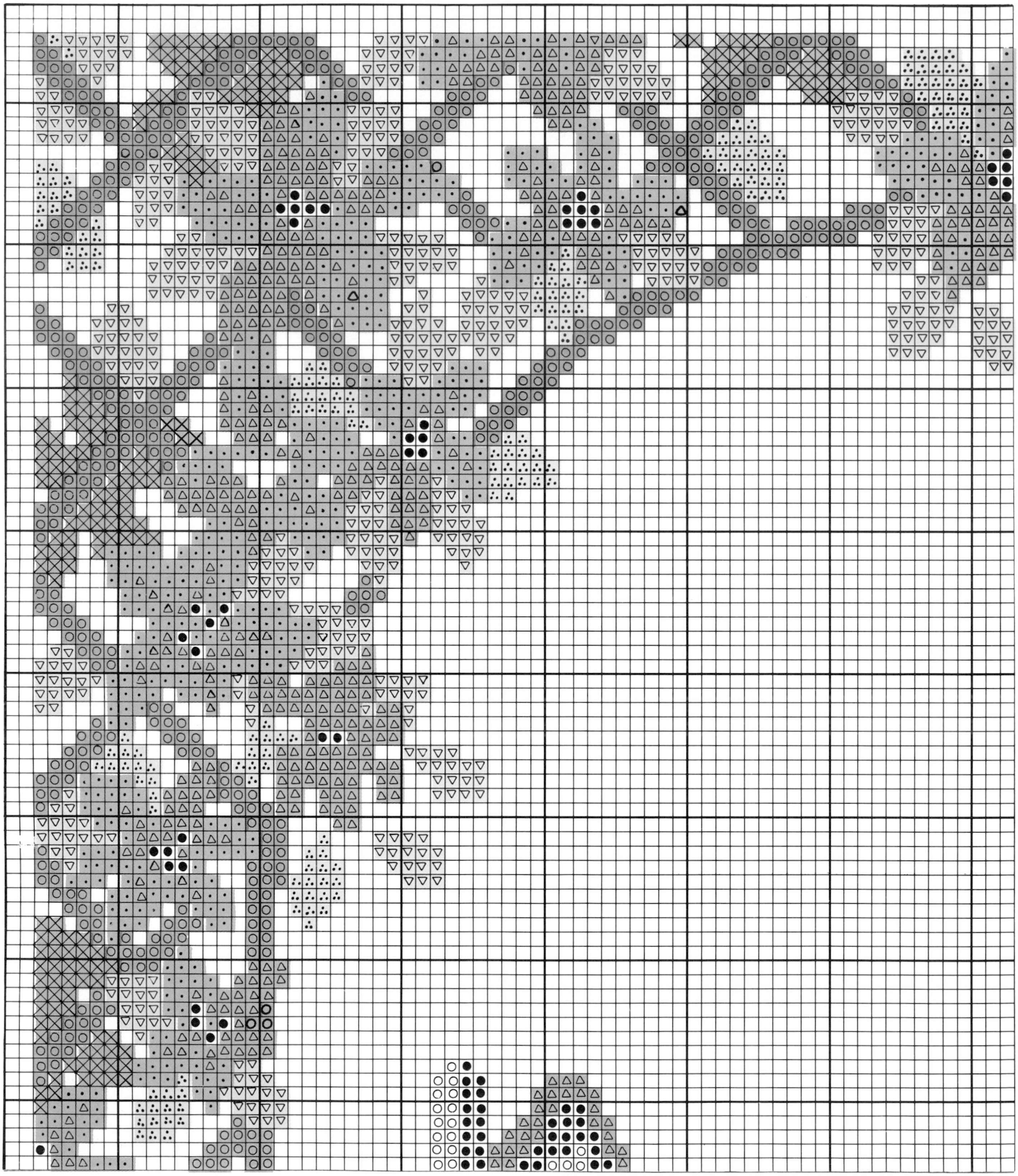

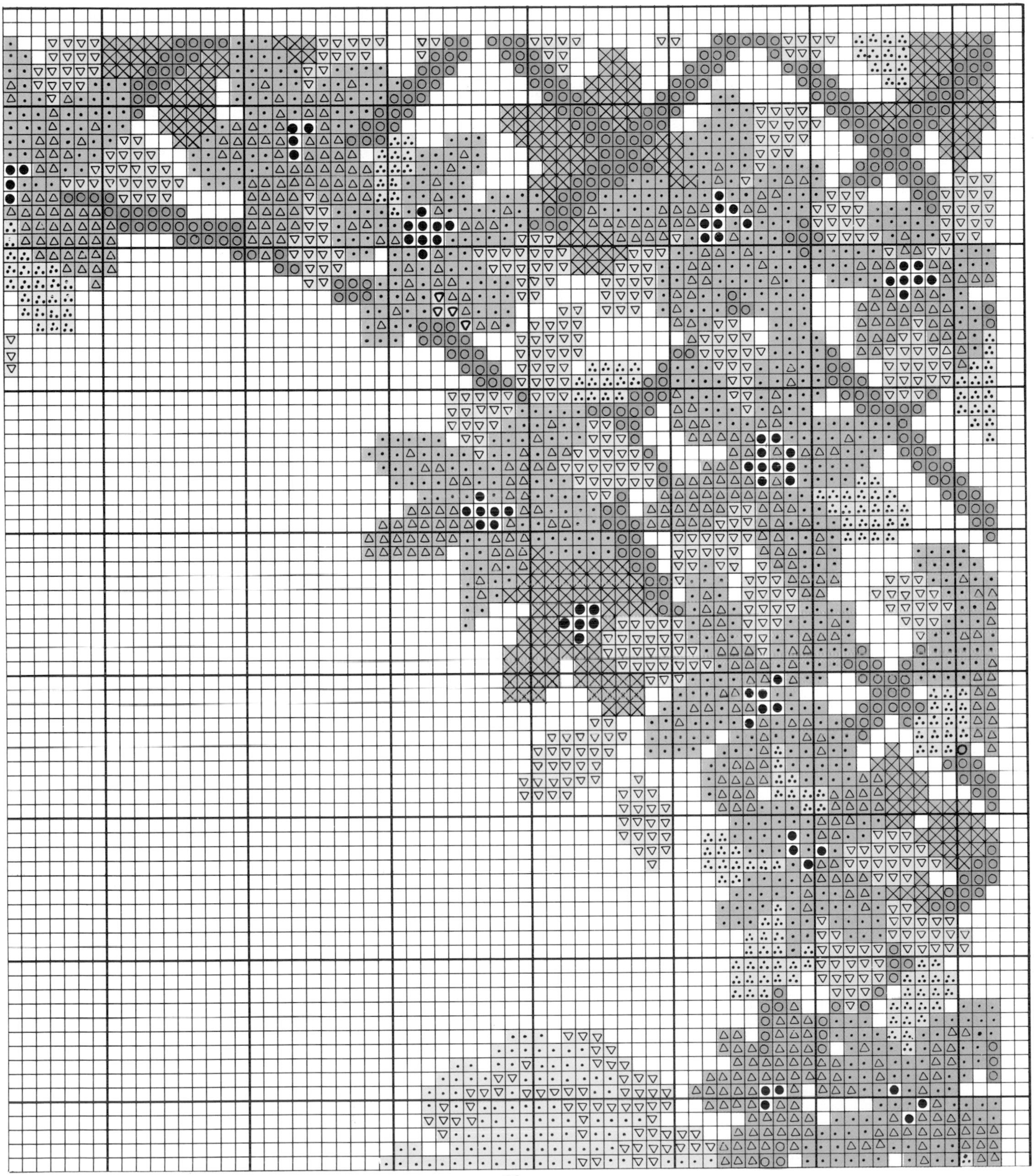

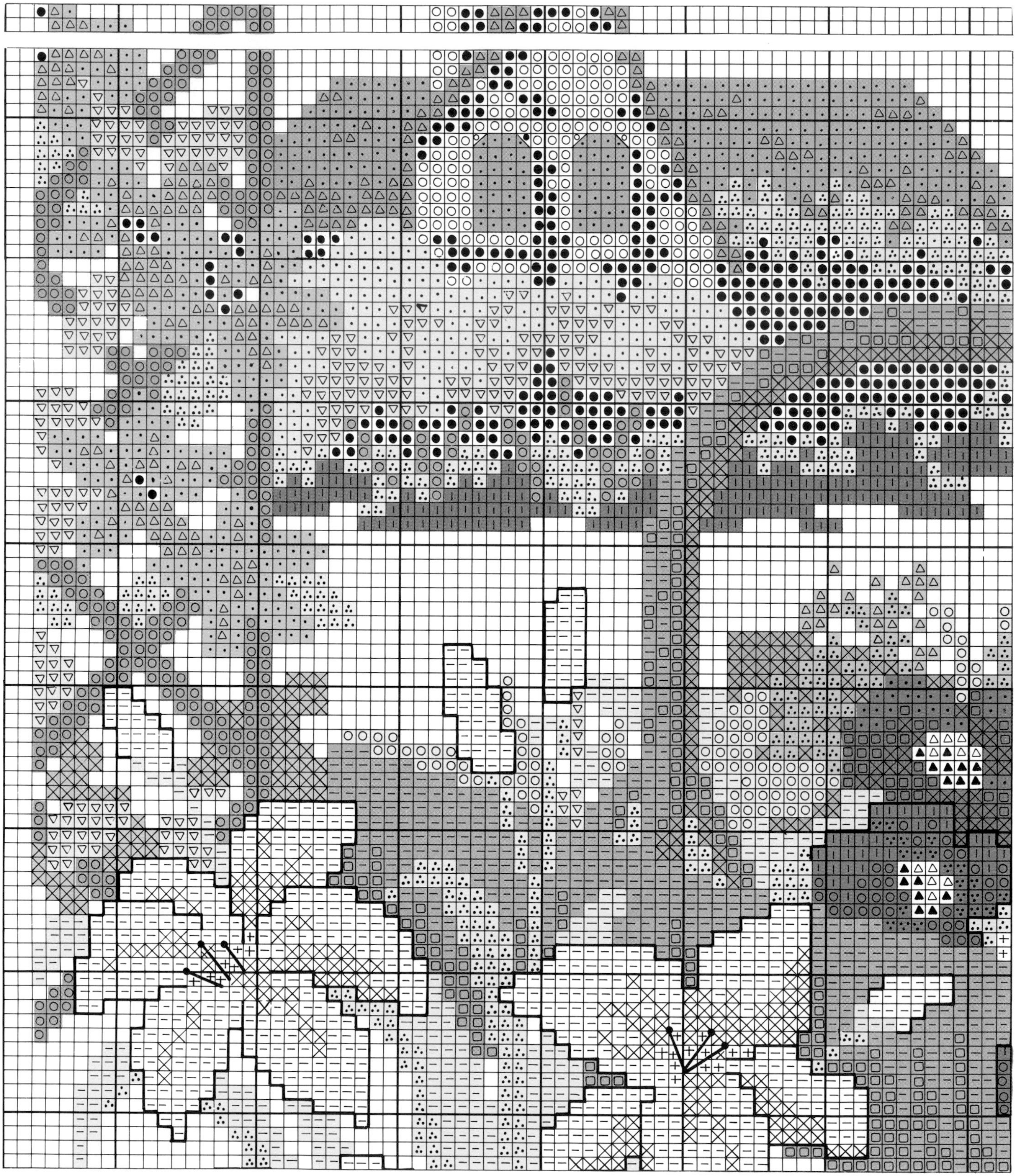

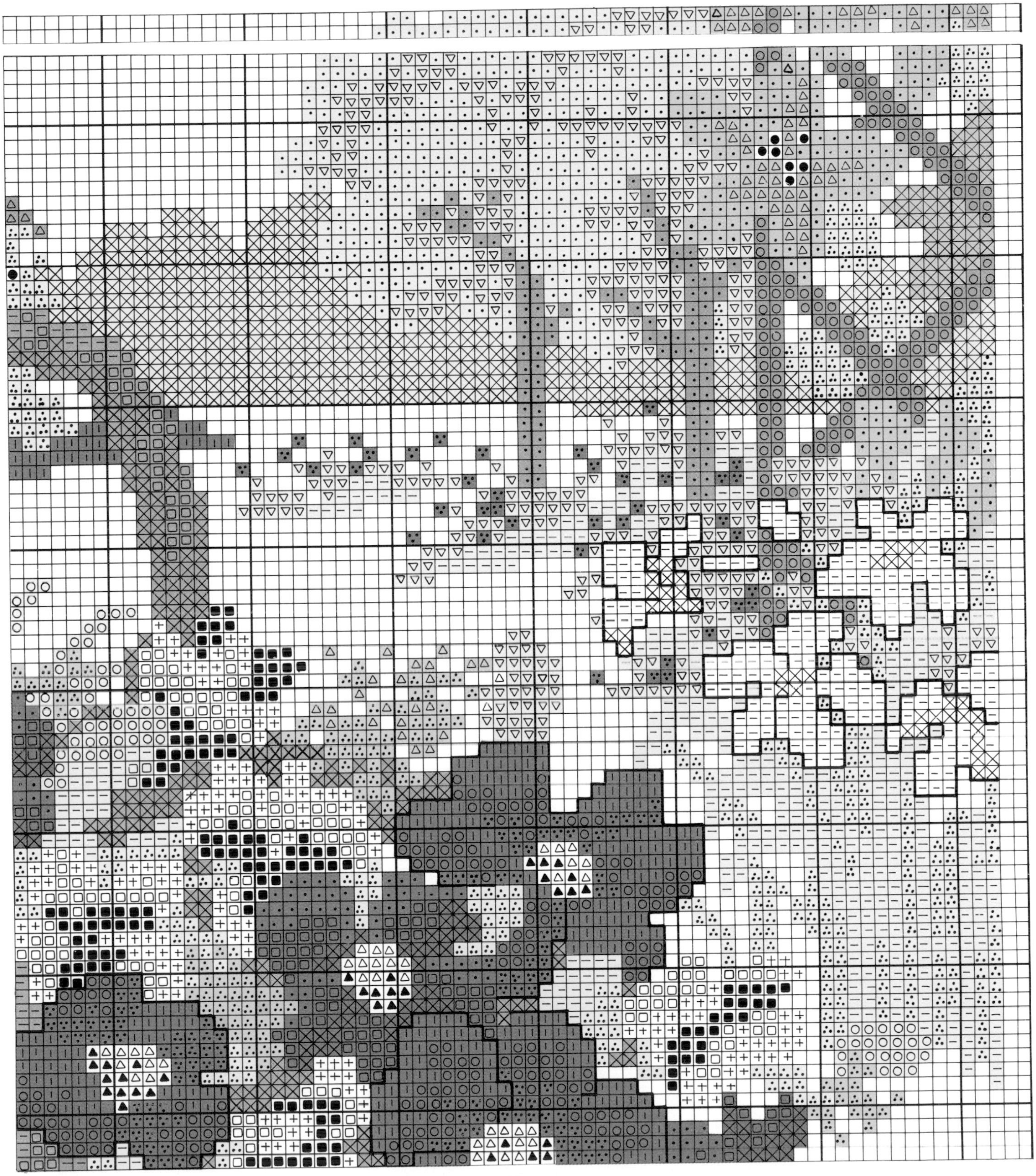

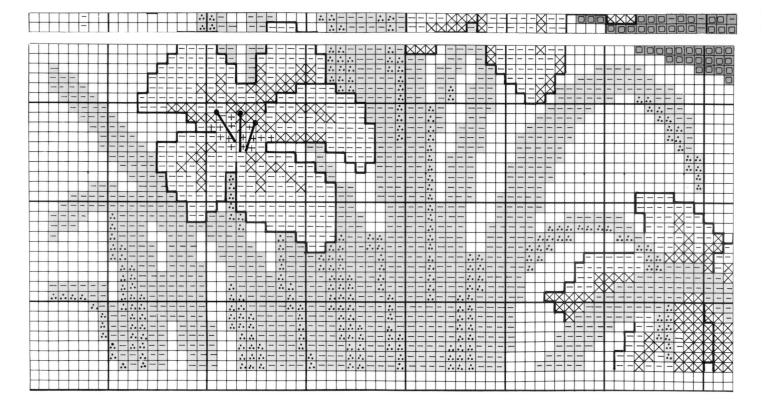

In My Mother's Garden

Stitched on cream Belfast Linen 32 over two threads, the finished design size is 8¾" x 12¾". The fabric was cut 15" x 19". More than one thread color represented by a single symbol on the code and graph indicates blending; note number of strands used.

FABRICS

FABRICS	DESIGN SIZES
Aida 11	12⅝" x 18⅝"
Aida 14	9⅞" x 14⅝"
Aida 18	7¾" x 11⅜"
Hardanger 22	6⅜" x 9¼"

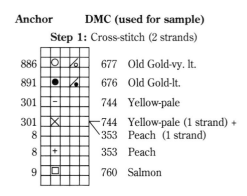

Anchor   DMC (used for sample)

Step 1: Cross-stitch (2 strands)

Anchor		DMC	(used for sample)
886	O /	677	Old Gold-vy. lt.
891	● /	676	Old Gold-lt.
301	−	744	Yellow-pale
301	X	744	Yellow-pale (1 strand) +
8		353	Peach (1 strand)
8	+	353	Peach
9	□	760	Salmon

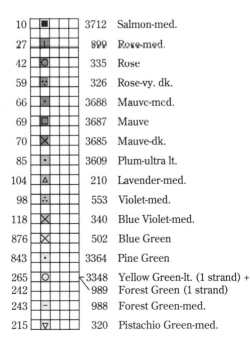

Stitch Count: 139 x 205

10	■	3712	Salmon-med.
27	I	899	Rose-med.
42	O	335	Rose
59	∴	326	Rose-vy. dk.
66	◼	3688	Mauve-med.
69	▣	3687	Mauve
70	✕	3685	Mauve-dk.
85	▨	3609	Plum-ultra lt.
104	△	210	Lavender-med.
98	∴	553	Violet-med.
118	✕	340	Blue Violet-med.
876	✕	502	Blue Green
843	·	3364	Pine Green
265	O	3348	Yellow Green-lt. (1 strand) +
242		989	Forest Green (1 strand)
243	–	988	Forest Green-med.
215	▽	320	Pistachio Green-med.

246	∴	319	Pistachio Green-vy. dk.
347	△	402	Mahogany-vy. lt.
338	▲	3776	Mahogany-lt.
363	–	436	Tan
370	□	434	Brown-lt.
357	✕	801	Coffee Brown-dk.
379	O	840	Beige Brown-med.
832	· ╱	612	Drab Brown-med.
898	△	611	Drab Brown-dk.

Step 2: Backstitch (1 strand)

59	▬	326	Rose-vy. dk. (rose flowers)
338	▬	3776	Mahogany-lt. (yellow flowers)

Step 3: French Knot (1 strand)

338	●	3776	Mahogany-lt.

Wings on Air Afghan

Stitched on Vanessa-Ann Afghan Weave 18 over two threads, the finished design size is 4" x 3⅛" for Design A, 4½" x 4¼" for Design B, 2½" x 1¾" for Design C, 4½" x 4½" for Design D. The fabric was cut 48" x 58". The width is seven whole blocks plus half a block on each side. The length is eight whole blocks plus half a block on each end. The stitch count of each block is 88 x 88. Heavy black lines surrounding each graph indicate block boundaries. Begin stitching in woven blocks as design dictates. Stitch five each of Design A, B, and D and six of C. See Diagram 1 for placement.

MATERIALS

Completed design pieces on Vanessa-Ann Afghan Weave 18*
¾ yard of light lavender fabric; matching thread
*see Suppliers

DIRECTIONS

1. Cut design piece to 46½" x 56½". Cut 2¼"-wide bias strips from lavender fabric, piecing as needed to equal 6 yards.

2. With right sides facing, sew bias to design piece, using ½" seam. Complete mitered corner binding; see General Instructions. Fold bias double to the wrong side, making a ⅝"-wide binding. Slipstitch in place, covering stitching line.

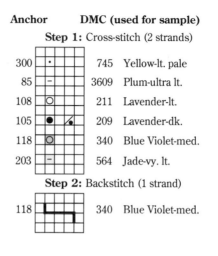

Anchor		DMC (used for sample)	
	Step 1: Cross-stitch (2 strands)		
300	·	745	Yellow-lt. pale
85	–	3609	Plum-ultra lt.
108	O	211	Lavender-lt.
105	● ╱	209	Lavender-dk.
118	O	340	Blue Violet-med.
203	–	564	Jade-vy. lt.
	Step 2: Backstitch (1 strand)		
118	⌐	340	Blue Violet-med.

Diagram 1

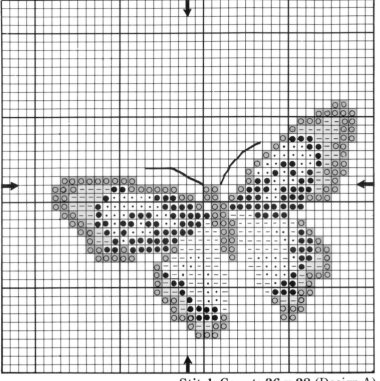

Stitch Count: 36 x 28 (Design A)

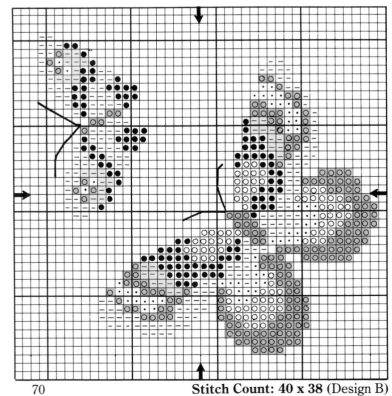

Stitch Count: 40 x 38 (Design B)

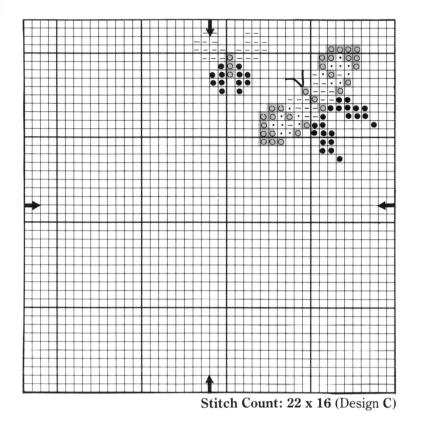

Stitch Count: 22 x 16 (Design C)

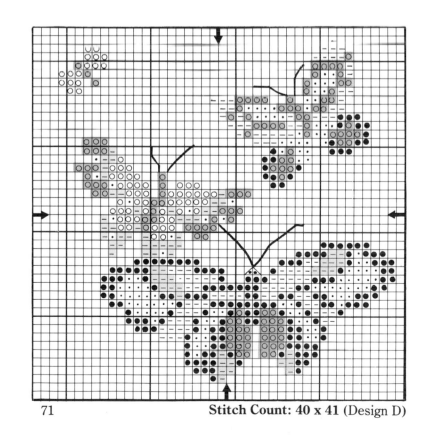

Stitch Count: 40 x 41 (Design D)

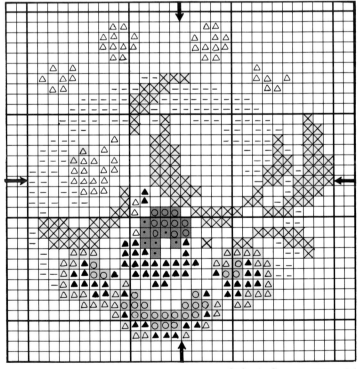

Garden Gazebo

Stitched on white Belfast Linen 32 over two threads, the finished design size is 1⅞" x 2". The fabric was cut 8" x 8".

FABRICS	DESIGN SIZES
Aida 11	2¾" x 2⅞"
Aida 14	2⅛" x 2¼"
Aida 18	1⅝" x 1¾"
Hardanger 22	1⅜" x 1⅜"

MATERIALS

Completed design on white Belfast Linen 32
Scrap of fleece
Mat board
Glue
7" x 14" wire gazebo*
4" x 3½" wooden bench
Dark green acrylic paint
Paintbrush
Green velvet leaves
White silk roses
Variety of dried miniature flowers
½ yard of 1½"-wide green wired ribbon
Florist's wire
Moss
Glue gun and glue
* see Suppliers

DIRECTIONS

1. Paint bench green. Allow to dry.

2. Make 3½" and 2½" circle patterns. Center 3½" pattern over design piece; cut. Cut one 2½" circle from fleece and two 2½" circles from mat board.

3. Glue fleece to front of one mat board circle. Center design piece and glue over fleece. Pull excess fabric to back, trimming bulk; glue. Glue remaining mat board circle to back over fabric.

4. Glue an assortment of velvet leaves, silk roses and dried flowers to top front of design piece as desired; see photo. Tie wired ribbon in a bow, leaving one 4" and one 2" tail. Center and glue to design piece and flowers. Set aside.

5. Wrap florist's wire back and forth across gazebo base. Weave and glue moss to gazebo at random. Glue wooden bench to moss inside gazebo. Apply remaining leaves and flowers as desired; see photo.

6. Loop long tail of wired bow on design piece over top center front of gazebo. Secure with glue.

Stitch Count: 30 x 31

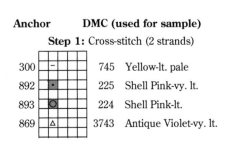

Anchor		DMC (used for sample)	
Step 1: Cross-stitch (2 strands)			
300	–	745	Yellow-lt. pale
892	•	225	Shell Pink-vy. lt.
893	O	224	Shell Pink-lt.
869	△	3743	Antique Violet-vy. lt.

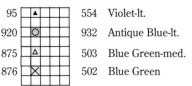

95	▲	554	Violet-lt.
920	O	932	Antique Blue-lt.
875	△	503	Blue Green-med.
876	✕	502	Blue Green

"They're fresh-picked,"
Mother might say, or,
"Because they're good
for you." What she
means is, "Because you
are special." Vegetables
from the home garden
nourish spirit as
well as body.

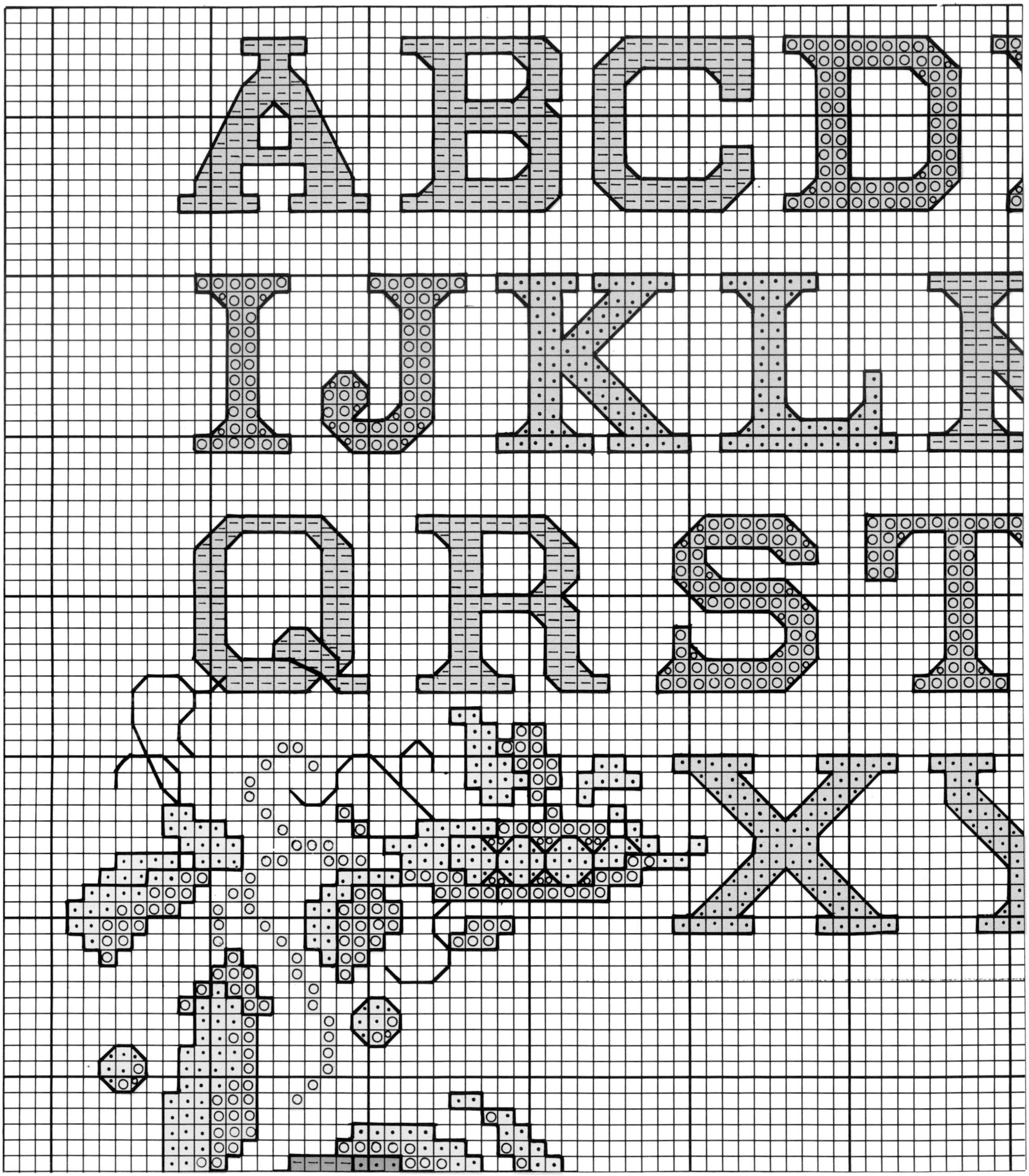

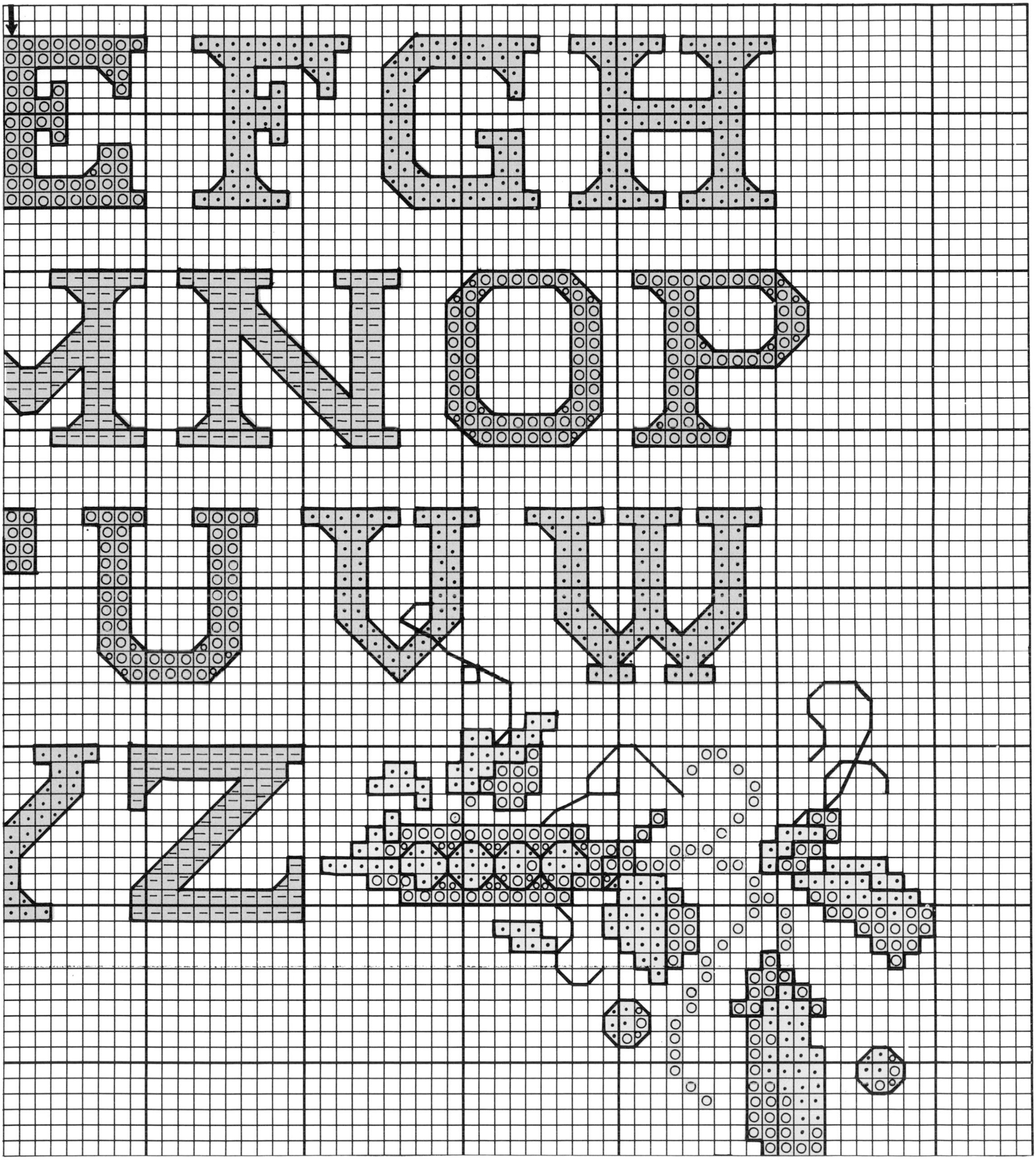

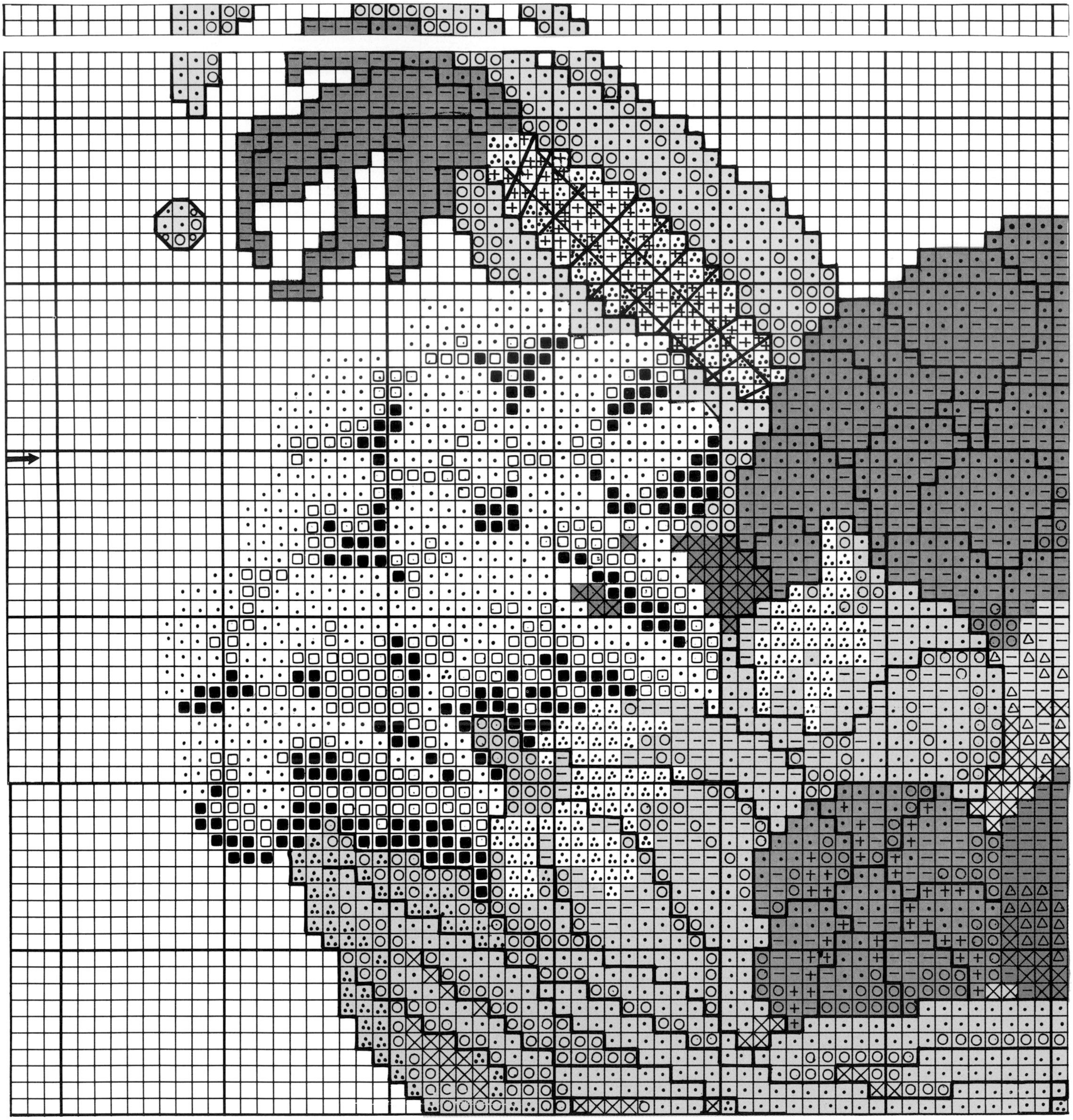

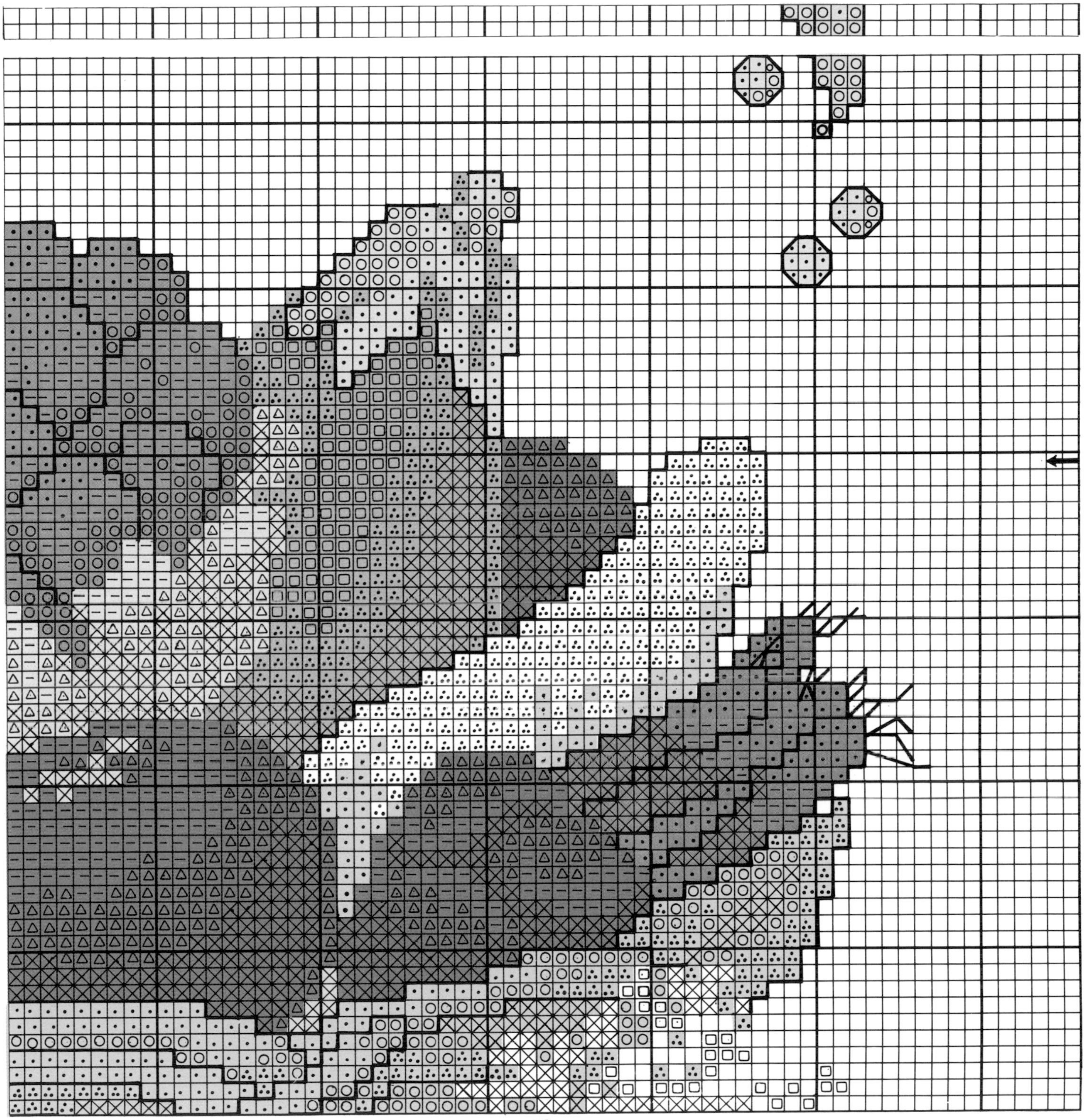

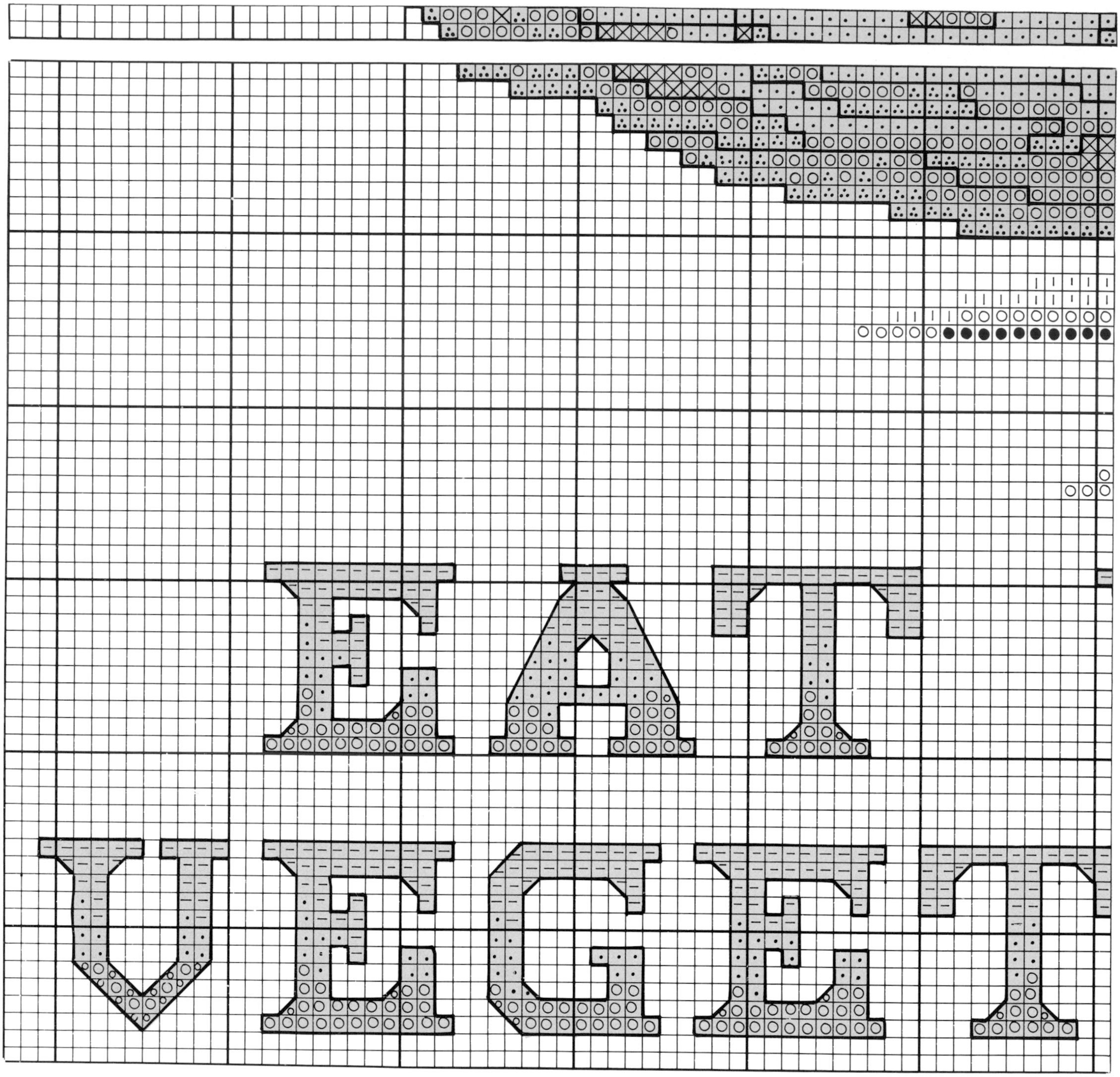
EAT
VEGET

Stitch Count: 125 x 191

Mother's Favorite Saying

Stitched on cracked wheat Murano 30 over two threads, the finished design size is 8⅜" x 12⅝". The fabric was cut 15" x 19". More than one thread color represented by a single symbol on the code and graph indicates blending; note number of strands used.

FABRICS
Aida 11
Aida 14
Aida 18
Hardanger 22

DESIGN SIZES
11⅜" x 17¼"
8⅞" x 13⅝"
7" x 10⅝"
5⅝" x 8⅝"

Anchor		DMC (used for sample)	
Step 1: Cross-stitch (2 strands)			
926	·		Ecru
301	+	744	Yellow-pale
306	∴	725	Topaz
316	I	971	Pumpkin
324	O	721	Orange Spice-med.
326	●	720	Orange Spice-dk.
11	▬	350	Coral-med.
19	▲	817	Coral Red-vy. dk.
20	✕	498	Christmas Red-dk.
970	▢	3726	Antique Mauve-dk.
869	+	3743	Antique Violet-vy. lt.
872	∴	3740	Antique Violet-dk.
872	✕	⌐3740	Antique Violet-dk. (1 strand) +
922		⌐930	Antique Blue-dk.(1 strand)
264	· ∕	472	Avocado Green-ultra lt.
266	O ∕	471	Avocado Green-vy. lt.

264	−	⌐472	Avocado Green-ultra lt. (1 strand) +
860		⌐3053	Green Gray (1 strand)
859	△	3052	Green Gray-med.
846	✕	3051	Green Gray-dk.
876	✕	502	Blue Green
859	·	⌐3052	Green Gray-med. (1 strand) +
876		⌐502	Blue Green (1 strand)
878	▢	501	Blue Green-dk.
879	■	500	Blue Green-vy. dk.
885	−	739	Tan-ultra vy. lt.
933	O	543	Beige Brown-ultra vy. lt.
264	✕	⌐472	Avocado Green-ultra lt. (1 strand) +
885		⌐739	Tan-ultra vy. lt. (1 strand)
307	· ∕	977	Golden Brown-lt.
306	− ∕	⌐725	Topaz (1 strand) +
307		⌐977	Golden Brown-lt. (1 strand)
308	O ∕	976	Golden Brown-med.
355	∴	975	Golden Brown-dk.
380	✕	839	Beige Brown-dk.

Anchor		DMC	
Step 2: Backstitch (1 strand)			
846		3051	Green Gray-dk. (peas, corn, green onions, eggplant)
307		977	Golden Brown-lt. (A, B, C, M, N, Q, R, Z)
308		976	Golden Brown-med. (F, G, H, K, L, V, W, X, Y, inside corn, saying)
355		975	Golden Brown-dk. (D, E, I, J, O, P, S, T, U, basket, brown onions, squash)
903		3032	Mocha Brown-med. (all else)

Home Tweet Home

The peas motif and alphabet are from "Mother's Favorite Saying" (pages 76–82). Stitched on cracked wheat Murano 30 over two threads, the finished design size varies with name stitched. The fabric was cut 19" x 19". Stitch name in DMC 977 Golden Brown-lt. and backstitch with DMC 976 Golden Brown-med. Center vertically and begin stitching first row 8⅛" above bottom edge of fabric.

MATERIALS

Completed design piece on cracked wheat Murano 30; matching thread
¾ yard of tan cotton fabric
⅜ yard of flannel
3" square of dark green fabric; matching thread
9" x 14" x ⅝" pine board
17½" of ¼"-thick wood molding
2¾" of ¼" round dowel
Craft knife
Mushroom bird
Spray adhesive
Staple gun and staples
Mat board
Dark green acrylic paint
Paintbrush
Small finishing nails
Glue gun and glue
Drill with ⅝" bit
Tracing paper
Dressmaker's pen

DIRECTIONS
All seams are ¼".

1. With design centered horizontally and last row of stitching 3½" above bottom edge, cut design piece to 13" square. Make patterns. Cut two gables from tan fabric and one from flannel. Cut a 2½"-wide circle from green fabric.

2. Mark 9" from bottom on each long edge of pine. Mark horizontal center on top front edge of pine. Connect marks, cutting on lines to make top edge of birdhouse; see Diagram 1. Mark 4½" from center bottom edge of pine. Drill a ⅝"-diameter hole ¼" deep.

3. Using pine as pattern, cut one birdhouse shape from mat board. Trim ¼" from all sides. Set aside.

4. Cut wood molding into one 8½" length and one 8¼" length. Paint each piece and dowel green. Allow to dry.

5. Fold edges of green circle to wrong side. Press. Center a mark 2¾" above last row of stitching on design piece. Center circle, wrong side down, on mark. Baste to design piece.

6. Draw scallops on wrong side of one gable piece ¼" above long gable edge. Layer flannel, then unmarked gable piece, then scallop-marked gable piece (wrong side up); baste. Carefully stitch along scallop-marked edge, using close stitch and pivoting at top of each scallop. Trim seam to ⅛", clipping corners at each pivot. Turn and press scalloped edge. Trace scallop pattern in parallel rows on right side of gable. Hand quilt or machine stitch along the lines.

7. Center design piece horizontally on pine board with last row of stitching 1¾" above bottom edge; mark edges. Attach design piece to pine with spray adhesive. Wrapping excess fabric to back, fold under at corners and staple around edges every 2". Center a mark 1" above last row of stitching. With craft knife, cut a ⅝" cross over hole in pine to allow for dowel placement. Fold cut fabric to inside of hole.

8. Center scalloped edge of gable 5" from top of birdhouse over design piece. Repeat Step 7 to attach. Center mat board on birdhouse back, stapling every 2" to cover.

9. For overhang, position 8¼" roof piece flush with back edge and point at top of covered pine piece. Drive two nails through top, attaching roof piece to birdhouse. Position 8½" roof piece flush with back edge and overlapping top edge of first roof piece. Nail to first roof piece and to birdhouse.

10. Apply glue to one end of dowel and insert into hole. Glue bird to dowel.

11. Apply additional coat of paint to tops of roof pieces as needed to cover nails. Allow to dry.

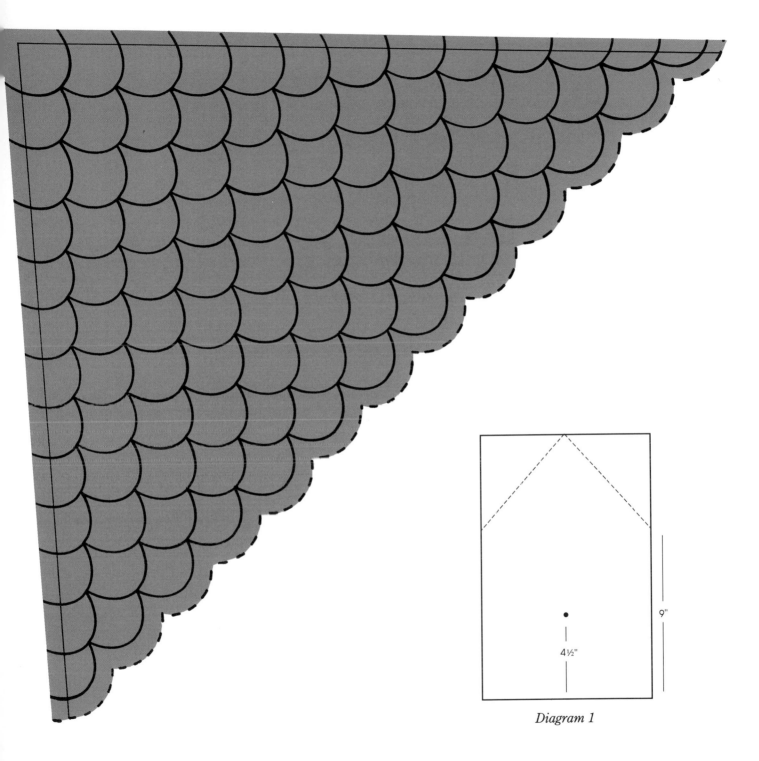

Diagram 1

9"

4½"

Fresh Carrots

Stitched on cracked wheat Murano 30 over two threads, the finished design size is 4⅝" x 2¼". The fabric was cut 14" x 13".

FABRICS	DESIGN SIZES
Aida 11	6⅜" x 3⅛"
Aida 14	5" x 2⅜"
Aida 18	3⅞" x 1⅞"
Hardanger 22	3⅛" x 1½"

MATERIALS (for one)

Completed design piece on cracked wheat Murano 30; matching thread
9" square of unstitched cracked wheat Murano 30
½ yard of aqua or tan polished cotton; matching thread
½ yard of fleece

DIRECTIONS
All seams are ¼".

1. Cut design piece to 7" x 8¼" with design centered. From unstitched Murano 30, cut one 7" x 8¼" piece for back. Cut two 7" x 8¼" pieces from fleece. From polished cotton, cut 1½"-wide bias strips, piecing as needed to equal 33".

2. Layer back (wrong side up), fleece and design piece (right side up). Zigzag all raw edges.

3. With right sides facing, sew bias to design piece, beginning at top left-hand corner. Complete mitered corner binding; see General Instructions. Do not trim extra binding length.

4. Fold bias double to back of pot holder. Slipstitch in place, covering stitching line. Turn under seam allowances on extended binding and slipstitch. For hanger, loop raw end to back, turn under and stitch at corner.

Anchor		DMC (used for sample)	
Step 1: Cross-stitch (2 strands)			
316	I	971	Pumpkin
324	O	721	Orange Spice-med.
326	●	720	Orange Spice-dk.
876	X	502	Blue Green
878	□	501	Blue Green-dk.

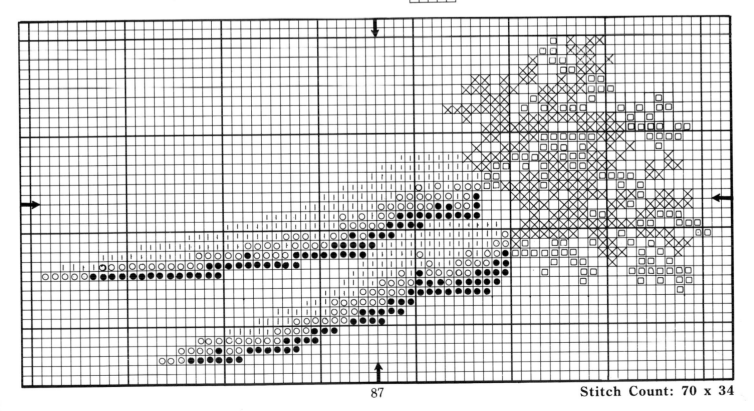

Stitch Count: 70 x 34

Cozy Coaster Basket

The motif is from "Mother's Favorite Saying" (pages 76–82). Stitched on cracked wheat Murano 30 over two threads, the finished design size is 7¼" x 6¼". The fabric was cut 16" x 13". More than one thread color represented by a single symbol on code and graph indicates blending; note number of strands used.

FABRICS	DESIGN SIZES
Aida 11	9⅞" x 8½"
Aida 14	7¾" x 6⅝"
Aida 18	6" x 5⅛"
Hardanger 22	5" x 4¼"

MATERIALS

Completed design piece on cracked wheat Murano 30; matching thread
¾ yard of unstitched cracked wheat Murano 30
½ yard of aqua polished cotton; matching thread
¼ yard of brown polished cotton; matching thread
¼ yard of lavender polished cotton; matching thread
¼ yard of rust polished cotton; matching thread
¾ yard of fleece
Tracing paper
Dressmaker's pen

DIRECTIONS
All seams are ¼".

1. Make patterns. Place basket front pattern over design piece; cut with design centered. Also cut one basket front each from unstitched Murano and fleece. Cut two basket backs from unstitched Murano and one from fleece. Also cut two 3" x 16½" pieces from unstitched Murano and one from fleece for handle. For coasters, cut eight 6" x 6" squares from unstitched Murano and four 6" x 6" squares from fleece.

2. Cut 1½"-wide aqua bias, piecing as needed to equal 2½ yards. Also cut 1"-wide bias each from brown, lavender and rust fabrics, piecing as needed to equal 24" each. Set aside.

3. Layer unstitched Murano basket front (wrong side up), fleece and design piece (right side up). Zigzag edges. Repeat with basket backs and handles.

4. Cut aqua bias into one 36" length, one 12½" length and two 16½" lengths. With right sides facing, align top long edge of design piece with 12½" bias length, mitering corners; see General Instructions. Fold bias double to back. Slipstitch, covering stitching line.

5. Place basket front over basket back, aligning edges. Zigzag edges of front to back. With right sides facing, stitch 36" bias length to basket edges, repeating Step 4.

6. With right sides facing and long raw edges aligned, stitch one 16½" bias length to each long edge of handle, repeating Step 4.

7. Zigzag short edges of handle. Mark 2" below point of basket back. Fold under seam allowance on one short handle edge and slipstitch to outside of basket back at mark. Slipstitch inside basket edge to handle.

8. Center a mark ¾" from top edge on inside of basket front. Slipstitch remaining short handle edge at mark. Slipstitch basket edge to handle.

9. To complete each coaster, sandwich a 6" x 6" fleece square between two 6" x 6" unstitched Murano squares. Zigzag edges. Attach one 24" bias strip to each coaster, repeating Step 4. Insert coasters into basket.

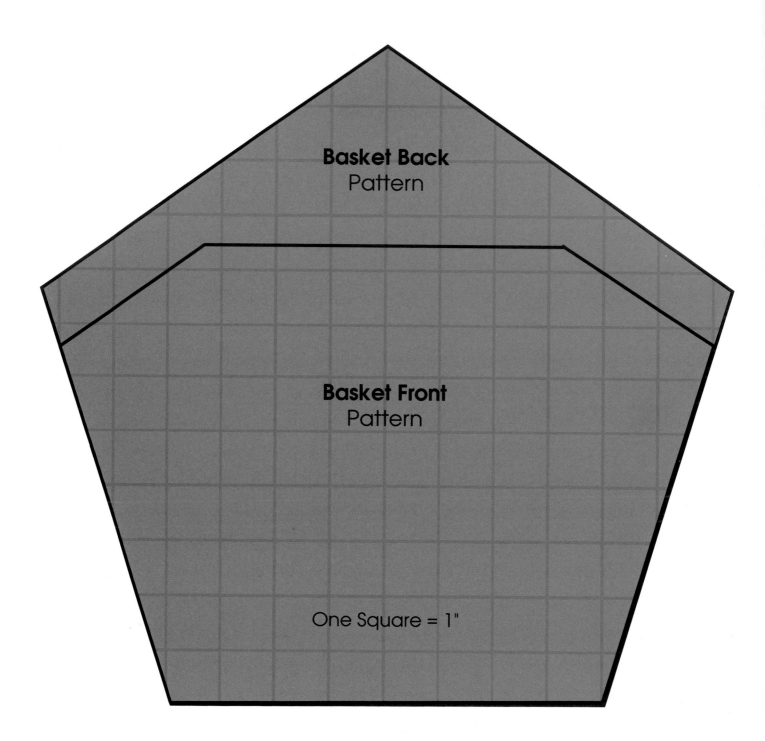

Basket Back
Pattern

Basket Front
Pattern

One Square = 1"

Mother Nature grows a garden of meadow blossoms. Her children of all ages find joy in picking wildflowers, splashing in a cool stream, or watching the antics of a playful rabbit.

The Peaceful Pasture

Stitched on celery green Linda 27 over two threads, the finished design size is 14½" x 12⅛". The fabric was cut 21" x 19".

FABRICS | **DESIGN SIZES**
Aida 11 | 17¾" x 14⅞"
Aida 14 | 13⅞" x 11⅝"
Aida 18 | 10⅞" x 9"
Hardanger 22 | 8⅞" x 7⅜"

Anchor   **DMC (used for sample)**

Step 1: Cross-stitch (2 strands)

Anchor			DMC	Color
1				White
292			3078	Golden Yellow-vy. lt.
366	S		951	Peach Pecan-lt.
25	O		3326	Rose-lt.
66			3688	Mauve-med.
69	X		3687	Mauve
42			3350	Dusty Rose-dk.
11			3328	Salmon-dk.
13	O		347	Salmon-vy. dk.
869	+		3743	Antique Violet-vy. lt.
872	%		3740	Antique Violet-dk.
158	I		775	Baby Blue-vy. lt.
159	v		3325	Baby Blue-lt.
121	.		794	Cornflower Blue-lt.
940	□		793	Cornflower Blue-med.
928	I		598	Turquoise-lt.
167	U		597	Turquoise
186	/		993	Aquamarine-lt.
876	△		502	Blue Green
214	.		368	Pistachio Green-lt.
215	::		320	Pistachio Green-med.
216	▼		367	Pistachio Green-dk.
246	□		319	Pistachio Green-vy. dk.
210	U		562	Jade-med.
212	●		561	Jade-vy. dk.
861	X		3363	Pine Green-med.
882	=		3773	Pecan-vy. lt.
914	▲		3772	Pecan-med.
903	M		3032	Mocha Brown-med.
905	□		3781	Mocha Brown-dk.
347	G		402	Mahogany-vy. lt.
349	◪		301	Mahogany-med.
900			3024	Brown Gray-vy. lt.
400	■		414	Steel Gray-dk.
401	::		413	Pewter Gray-dk.

Step 2: Backstitch (1 strand)

236		3799	Pewter Gray-vy. dk.

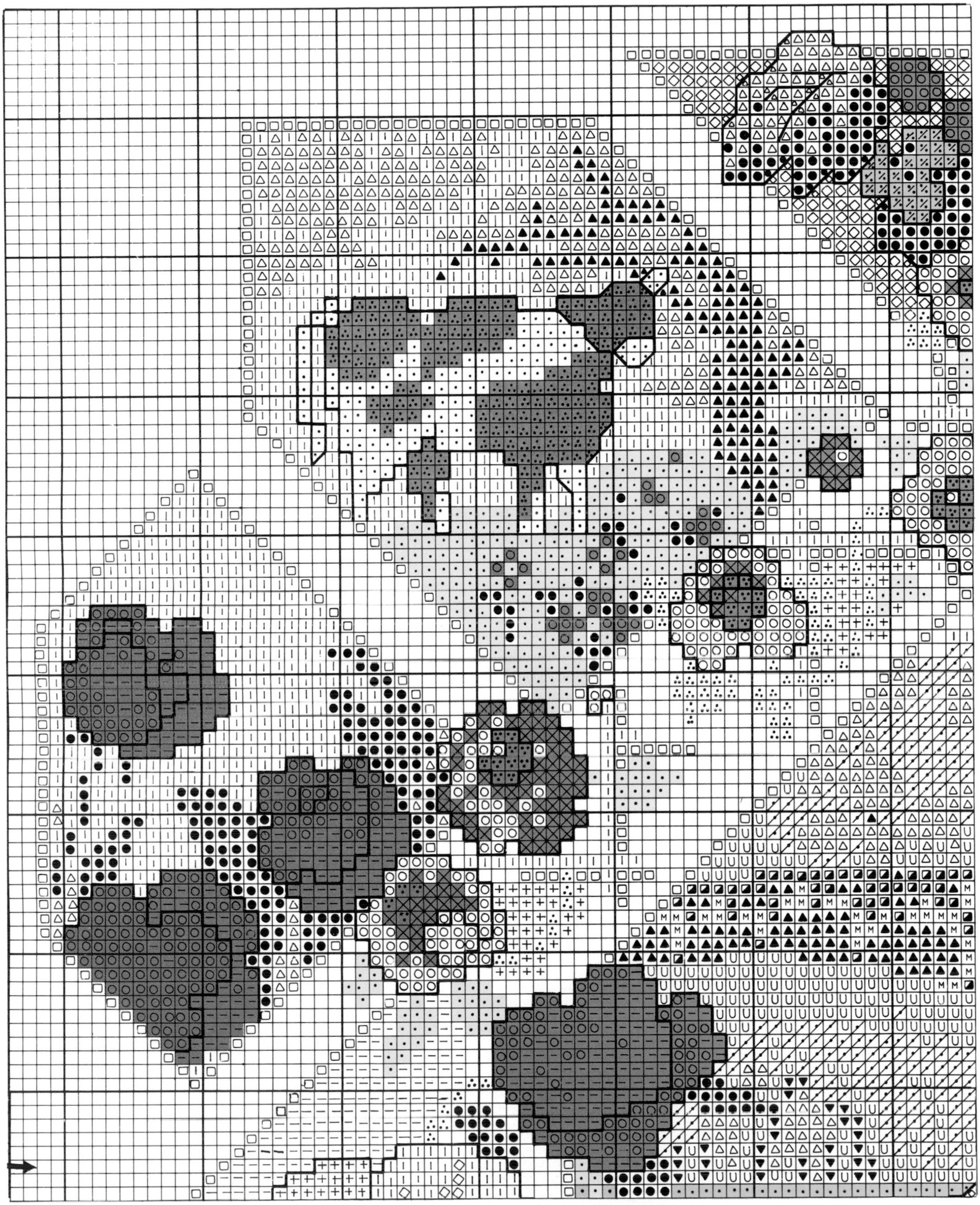

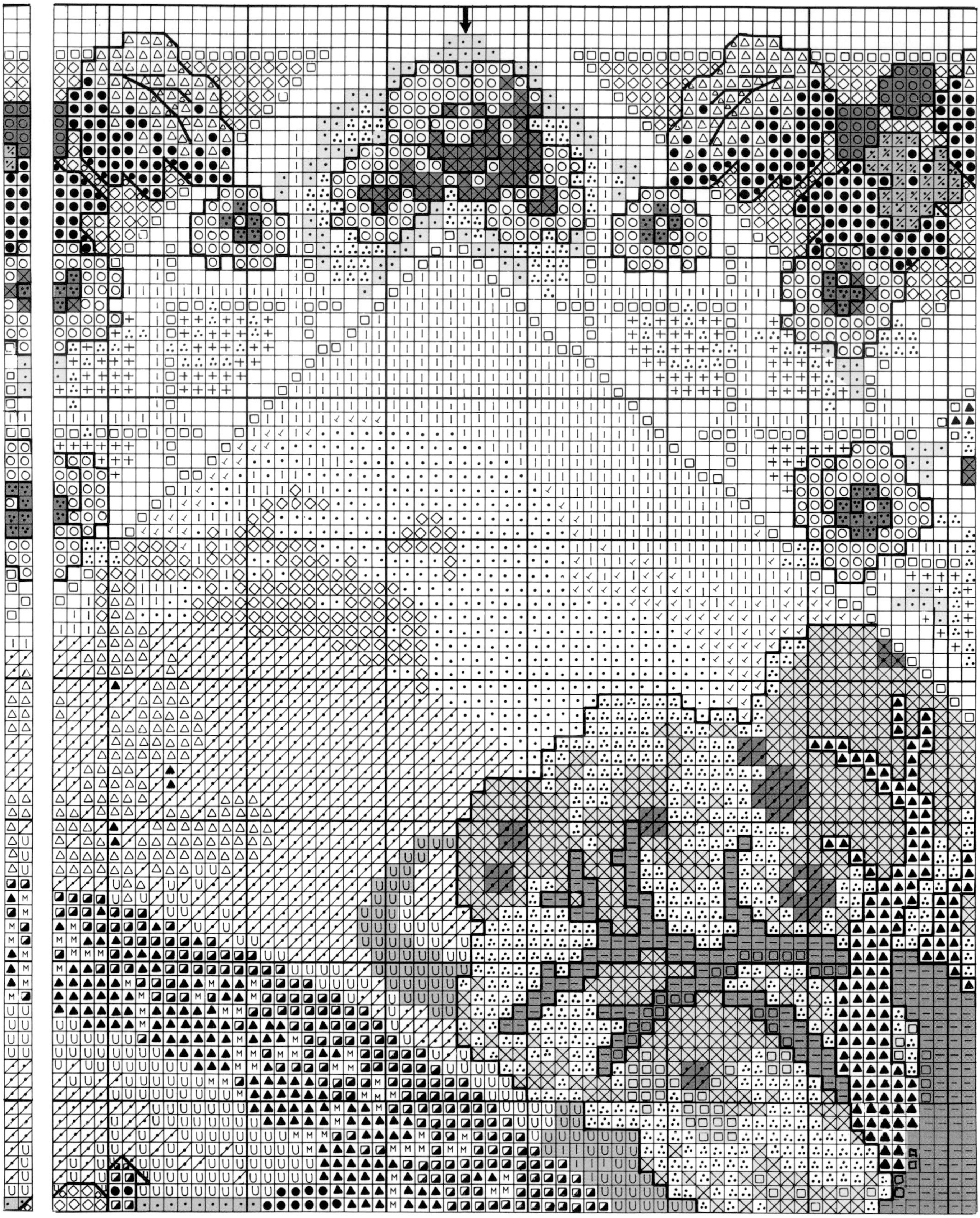

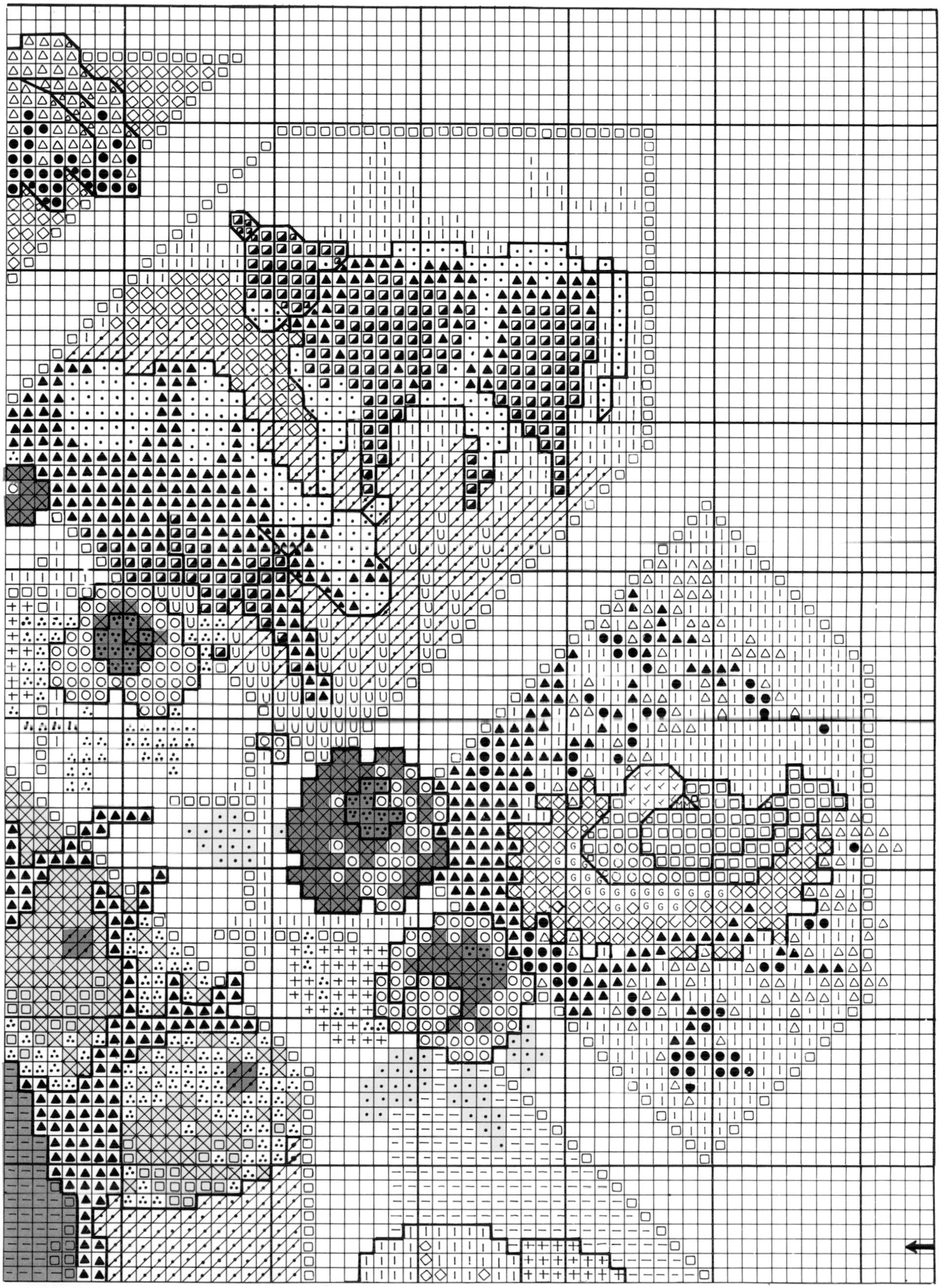

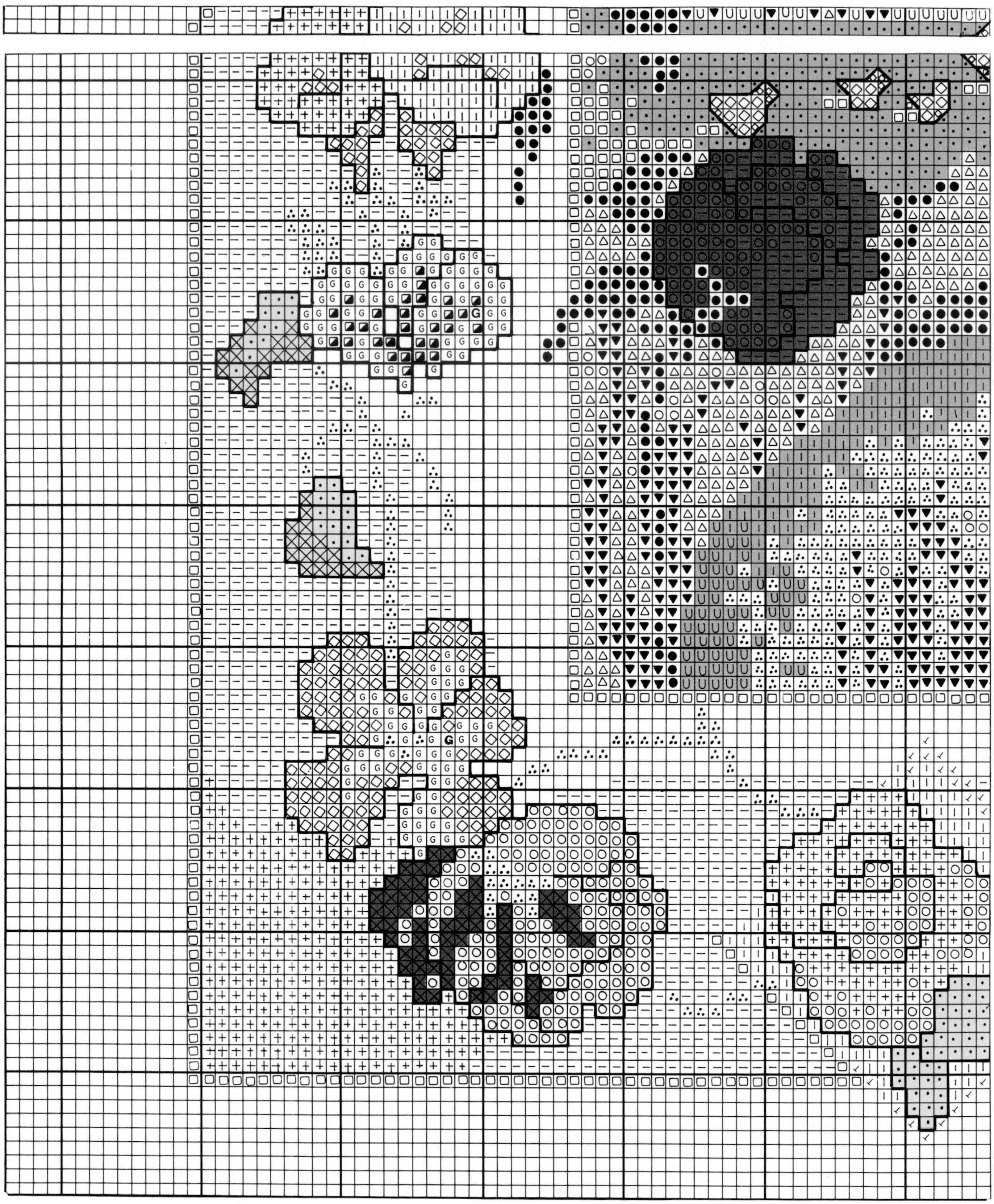

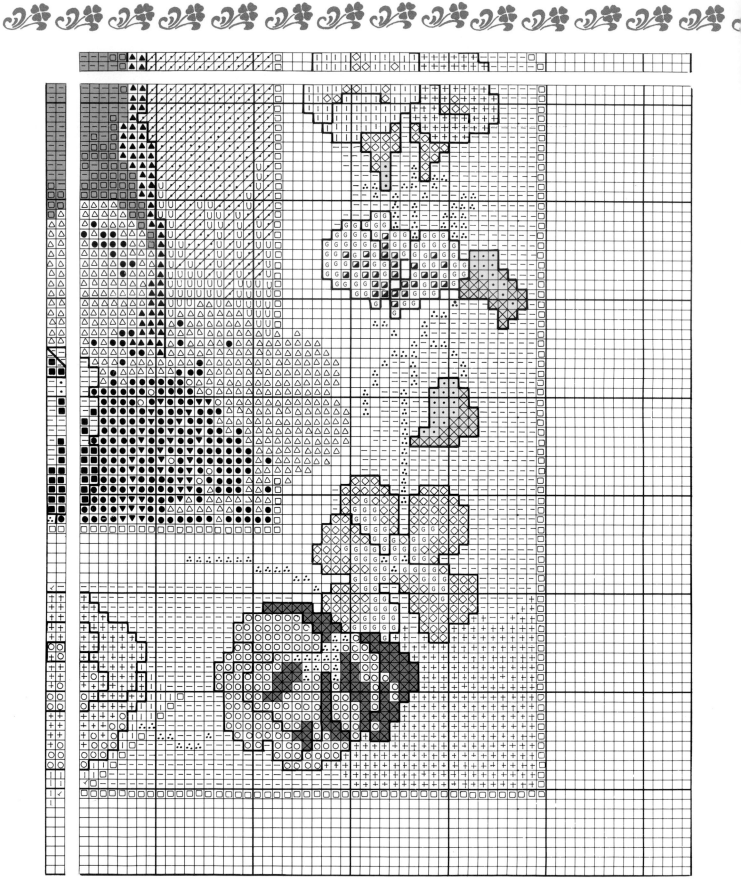

Stitch Count: 195 x 163

THE PEACEFUL PASTURE

Soft Wings

The motif is from "The Peaceful Pasture" (pages 94–100); the finished design will be on the bias. Stitched on celery green Linda 27 over two threads, the finished design size is 3⅛" x 3¼". The fabric was cut 8" x 9".

FABRICS / DESIGN SIZES

FABRICS	DESIGN SIZES
Aida 11	4" x 4"
Aida 14	3⅛" x 3⅛"
Aida 18	2⅜" x 2⅜"
Hardanger 22	1" x 1"

MATERIALS

Completed design piece on celery green Linda 27
One 2" x 7" piece of unstitched celery green Linda 27 for back of design piece
¾ yard of 45"-wide polished cotton fabric for pillow; matching thread
¼ yard of 45"-wide matching cotton fabric; matching thread
½ yard of ⅛"-wide cording
One 2" x 7" scrap of flannel
Polyester stuffing

DIRECTIONS

1. Turn completed design piece on bias and cut 2" x 7", with design centered. From polished cotton fabric, cut two 11" x 12" pieces. From cotton fabric, cut 1"-wide bias strips, piecing as needed to equal ½ yard. Make corded piping. Cut piping into two equal lengths.

2. Zigzag flannel to wrong side of design piece. Press if needed. With right sides facing and raw edges aligned, stitch one length of piping on each long edge of design piece. Repeat to stitch design piece to back, following stitching line of piping. Turn.

3. For pillow, with right sides facing and raw edges aligned, stitch polished cotton fabric pieces together, leaving an opening for turning. Turn. Stuff moderately. Slipstitch opening closed.

4. Wrap design piece around middle of pillow, easing fullness; see photo. Turn under seam allowance of one end of design piece. Insert remaining raw end and slipstitch securely.

Meadow Reflections

Stitched on antique tan Linen 28 over two threads, the finished design size is 11⅞" x 6". The fabric was cut 21" x 26".

FABRICS
Aida 11
Aida 14
Aida 18
Hardanger 22

DESIGN SIZES
15⅛" x 7⅝"
11⅞" x 6"
9¼" x 4⅝"
7⅝" x 3⅞"

MATERIALS

Completed design piece on antique tan Linen 28
Professionally cut mat; see Step 1 of Directions
15" x 20" mirror
Double-sided tape
Masking tape
Dressmaker's pen

DIRECTIONS

1. Have a professional framer cut a 15" x 20" mat board with a 7" x 12" window, centered.

2. On flat surface, center mat on wrong side of design piece and trace window edge. Then draw smaller window 1" inside first window. Cut along smaller window's pen line. Clip fabric from window to remaining pen line at ⅜" intervals.

3. On wrong side of mat, place small strips of double-sided tape around window and outside edge of mat. Center right side of mat over wrong side of design. Fold clipped edges of design piece over window edges first, then outside edges over outside edges of mat, pulling taut. Secure with masking tape. Place mat in frame first, then mirror. Secure according to frame manufacturer's instructions or have professional framer complete.

Anchor		DMC (used for sample)	
Step 1: Cross-stitch (2 strands)			
292	◇	3078	Golden Yellow-vy. lt.
25	○	3326	Rose-lt.
69	✕	3687	Mauve
869	+	3743	Antique Violet-vy. lt.
872	⚹	3740	Antique Violet-dk.
158	I	775	Baby Blue-vy. lt.
159	✓	3325	Baby Blue-lt.
214	· ╱	368	Pistachio Green-lt.
215	∴ ╱	320	Pistachio Green-med.
861	✕	3363	Pine Green-med.
347	G	402	Mahogany-vy. lt.
349	◪	301	Mahogany-med.
Step 2: Backstitch (1 strand)			
236	└	3799	Pewter Gray-vy. dk.

105

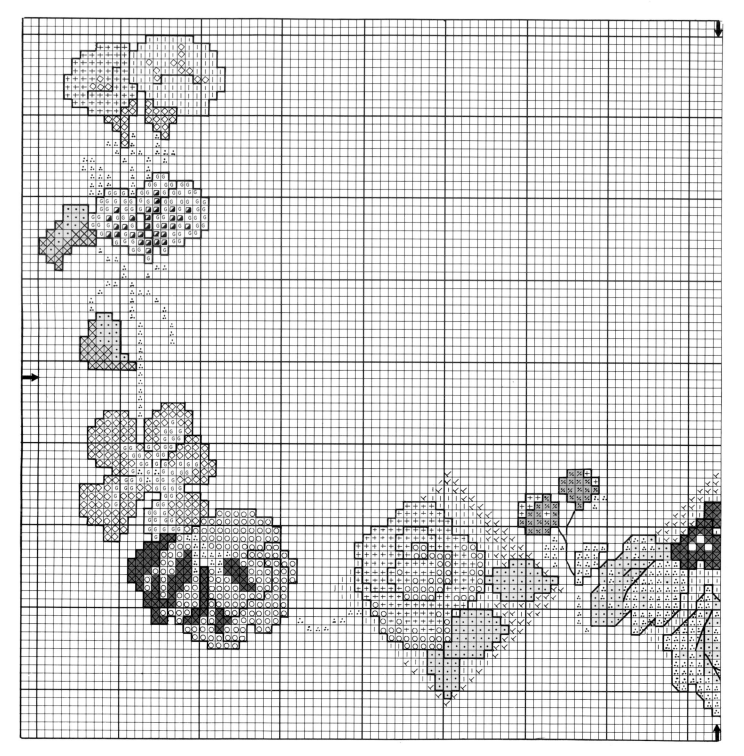

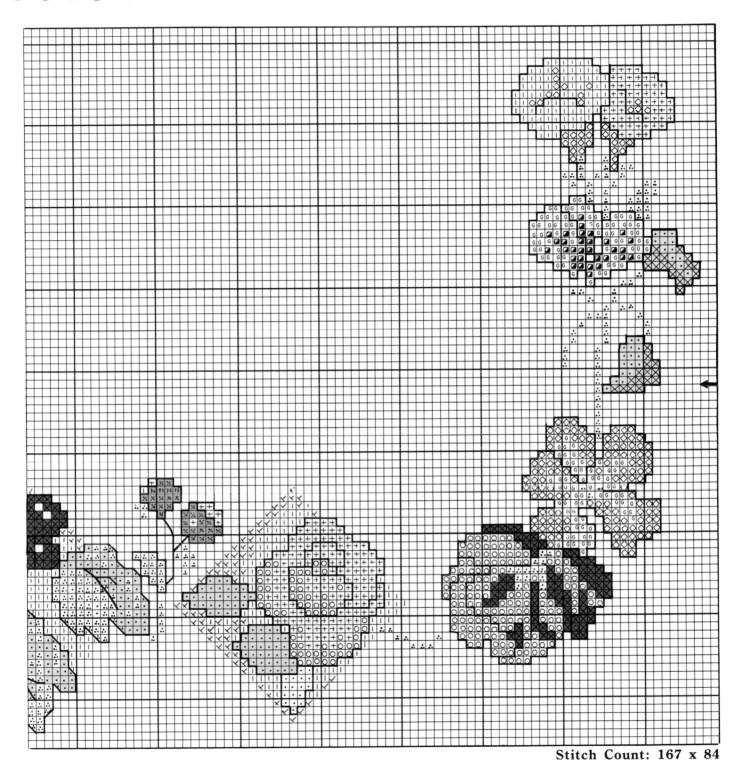

Stitch Count: 167 x 84

Enduring Lily

Stitched on cream Belfast Linen 32 over two threads, the finished design size is 1" x 1⅛". The fabric was cut 6" x 6".

FABRICS

FABRICS	DESIGN SIZES
Aida 11	1½" x 1⅝"
Aida 14	1⅛" x 1¼"
Aida 18	⅞" x 1"
Hardanger 22	¾" x ⅞"

MATERIALS

Completed design piece on cream Belfast Linen 32
Purchased ceramic jar with lid
Scrap of fleece
Mat board
Glue gun and glue
Button

DIRECTIONS

1. Make 1⅜"-wide circle from mat board and one from fleece. Center circle over design piece; cut.

2. Glue fleece to mat board. Center design piece over fleece. Fold excess fabric to back, trimming bulk; glue.

3. Glue button to purchased jar lid as desired.

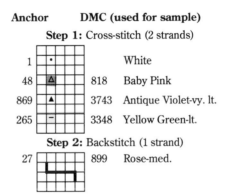

Anchor		DMC (used for sample)	
Step 1: Cross-stitch (2 strands)			
1	·	White	
48	△	818	Baby Pink
869	▲	3743	Antique Violet-vy. lt.
265	−	3348	Yellow Green-lt.
Step 2: Backstitch (1 strand)			
27		899	Rose-med.

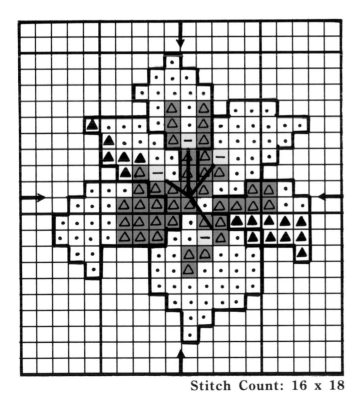

Stitch Count: 16 x 18

*A flowery dinosaur
inhabits a child's
garden of numbers.
Familiar rhymes make
remembering as easy
as riding a stick horse!*

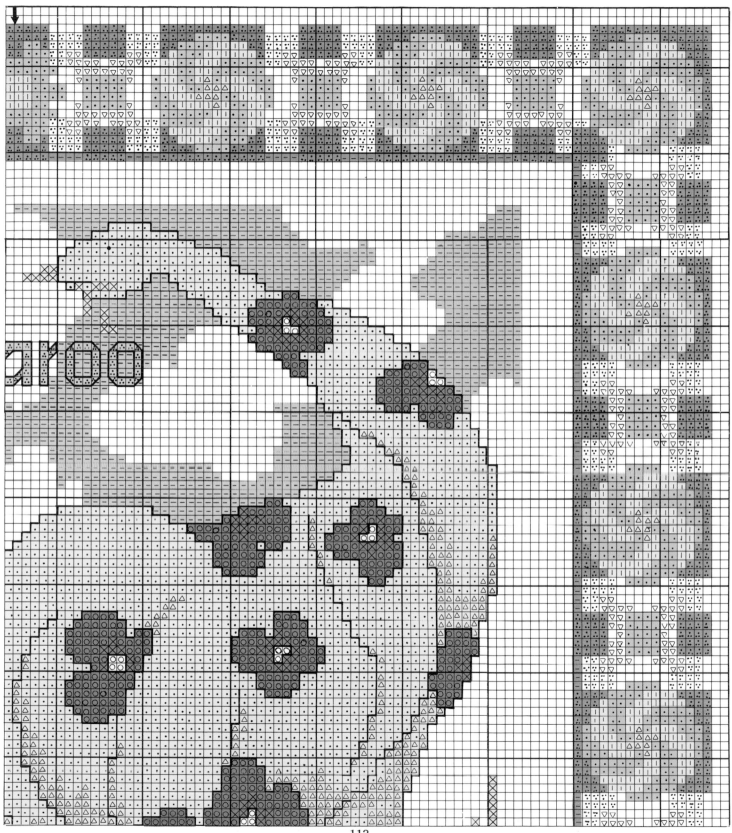

candle
sticks

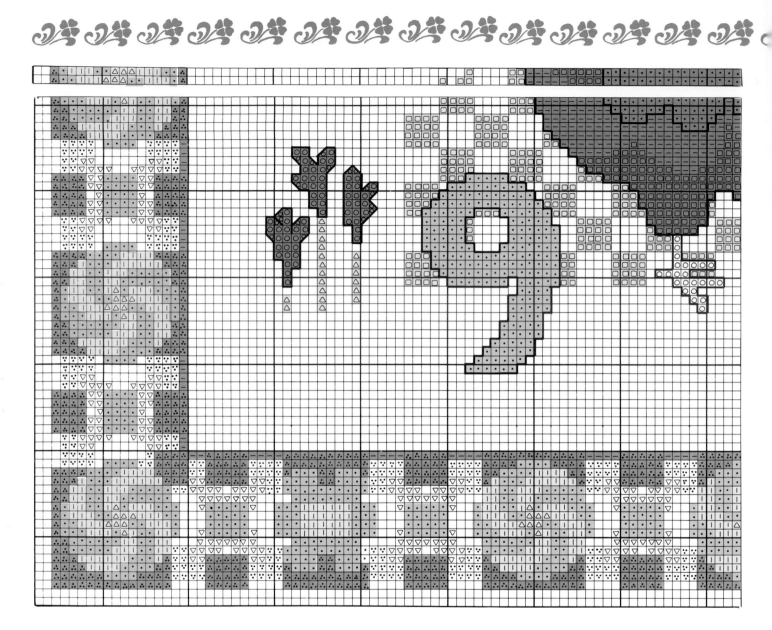

Counting Dinosaur

Stitched on white Hardanger 22 over two threads, the finished design size is 14¾" x 22". The fabric was cut 21" x 28".

FABRICS	DESIGN SIZES
Aida 11	14¾" x 21⅞"
Aida 14	11⅝" x 17¼"
Aida 18	9" x 13⅜"
Hardanger 22	7⅜" x 11"

The preferred spelling of "buckaroo" is with a k, as it appears on the chart.

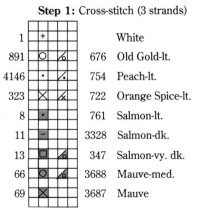

Anchor			DMC	(used for sample)

Step 1: Cross-stitch (3 strands)

Anchor			DMC	
1	+			White
891	O	◪	676	Old Gold-lt.
4146	·	◪	754	Peach-lt.
323	X	◪	722	Orange Spice-lt.
8	▪		761	Salmon-lt.
11	−		3328	Salmon-dk.
13	▣	◪	347	Salmon-vy. dk.
66	◉	◪	3688	Mauve-med.
69	✕		3687	Mauve

116

Stitch Count: 162 x 241

95		554	Violet-lt.
98		553	Violet-med.
101		327	Antique Violet-vy. dk.
128		800	Delft-pale
128		800	Delft-pale (1 strand)
940		792	Cornflower Blue-dk.
203		564	Jade-vy. lt.
208		563	Jade-lt.
208		563	Jade-lt. (1 strand)
210		562	Jade-med.
212		561	Jade-vy. dk.
933		543	Beige Brown-ultra vy. lt. (1 strand)

942		738	Tan-vy. lt.
363		436	Tan
882		407	Pecan
903		3032	Mocha Brown-med.
399		318	Steel Gray-lt.
400		414	Steel Gray-dk.

Step 2: Backstitch (1 strand)

236		3799	Pewter Gray-vy. dk.

Step 3: French Knot (1 strand)

236		3799	Pewter Gray-vy. dk.

117

Stitch Count: 52 x 62

Fat Red Hen

The motif is from "Counting Dinosaur" (pages 112–117); center words under hen. Stitched on Floba 25 over two threads, the finished design size is 4⅛" x 5". The fabric was cut 11" x 11".

FABRICS
Aida 11
Aida 14
Aida 18
Hardanger 22

DESIGN SIZES
4¾" x 5⅝"
3¾" x 4½"
2⅞" x 3½"
2⅜" x 2⅞"

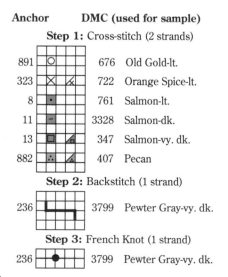

Anchor		DMC (used for sample)	
Step 1: Cross-stitch (2 strands)			
891	O	676	Old Gold-lt.
323	X ✗	722	Orange Spice-lt.
8	·	761	Salmon-lt.
11	■	3328	Salmon-dk.
13	▣ ◢	347	Salmon-vy. dk.
882	∷ ◿	407	Pecan
Step 2: Backstitch (1 strand)			
236		3799	Pewter Gray-vy. dk.
Step 3: French Knot (1 strand)			
236	●	3799	Pewter Gray-vy. dk.

119

Mother's Memories

The motif is from "Counting Dinosaur" (page 112). Stitched on dirty linen Linda 27 over two threads, the finished design size is 10¼" x 8½". Begin stitching 3" from top and left raw edge, using motif in upper left corner of graph and repeating as needed; see photo. The fabric was cut 18" x 16".

FABRICS	DESIGN SIZES
Aida 11	12⅝" x 10⅜"
Aida 14	9⅞" x 8⅛"
Aida 18	7¾" x 6⅜"
Hardanger 22	6⅜" x 5⅛"

MATERIALS

Completed design piece on dirty linen Linda 27
48 red beads (#00968)*
Wooden frame with 11½" x 9½" window
Two 12" x 10" pieces of mat board
Two 12" x 10" pieces of fleece
Glue
*see Suppliers

Cowpoke Star 🌸

The motif is from "Counting Dinosaur" (pages 112–117). Stitched on Rustico 14, the finished design size is 3⅛" x 4⅝". The fabric was cut 10" x 11".

FABRICS	DESIGN SIZES
Aida 11	4" x 5¾"
Aida 14	3⅛" x 4⅝"
Aida 18	2⅜" x 3½"
Hardanger 22	2" x 2⅞"

MATERIALS

Completed design piece on Rustico 14
Wooden box*
¼ yard of fleece
Three ½" red star buttons
Blue thread
Mat board
Glue gun and glue
* see Suppliers

DIRECTIONS

1. Have a professional framer cut two 12" x 10" mat board pieces, one with 7½" x 5¼" window and one with 6¾" x 4¾" window, each centered.

2. Stitch four beads in center of three round motifs at each corner; see photo.

3. Cut design piece to 14" x 12" with design centered. Find center of design piece; cut out 5¾" x 3¾" window; see Diagram 1. Cut 7½" x 5¼" window from center of fleece pieces. Glue fleece to mat board with 7½" x 5¼" window.

4. On design piece, slit corners of window diagonally to 7½" x 5¼"; see Diagram 2. Center design piece over fleece-covered mat board, folding excess to back; glue.

5. Insert design piece into frame. Then insert mat board with 6¾" x 4¾" window, photograph and frame backing. Secure according to frame manufacturer's instructions or have professional framer complete.

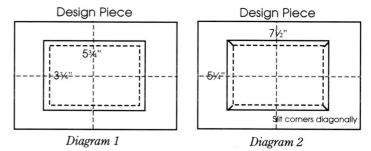

Diagram 1   *Diagram 2*

DIRECTIONS

1. To complete model, place buttons as desired; see photo. Then zigzag around outer edges of design piece. Cut two fleece pieces and one mat board piece to match insert.

2. Glue fleece pieces to mat board. Center design piece over fleece, folding excess fabric to back; glue. Glue design piece right side up to insert. Place in box lid.

Molly is a country girl and when she dresses up, she does it with simple things – homegrown posies, for example. Let her charm her way into your heart!

Doll Body

MATERIALS

Porcelain doll parts*
⅛ yard of white fabric; matching thread
Polyester stuffing
*see Suppliers

DIRECTIONS
All seams are ¼".

1. Make Doll Body patterns. Cut Doll Body pieces from white fabric according to patterns.

2. With right sides facing, fold one arm piece in half to equal 1⅜" wide. Stitch long seam only; do not turn. Position porcelain arm with hand down and insert into fabric arm. With side seam aligned with porcelain underarm and ¼" of fabric above groove on upper porcelain arm, secure fabric to porcelain by tying thread tightly around the groove; Diagram 1. Pull the arm through, turning fabric. Stuff fabric portion of arm. Slipstitch opening closed. Repeat for remaining arm.

3. To make legs, fold one leg piece in half to equal 1¾" at top. Stitch long seam only; do not turn. Repeat Step 2 using fabric legs and porcelain feet, aligning back seam of fabric with back of porcelain leg. Do not slipstitch opening closed.

4. Sew darts in body pieces according to patterns. With heel placed on right side of back piece, align raw edge of one upper leg with bottom raw edge of back piece and stitch; Diagram 2. Repeat for remaining leg. With right sides facing and legs sandwiched between, stitch front and back together, leaving a 1¾" opening at top. Pull legs through, turning fabric. Stuff body firmly. Slipstitch opening closed.

5. Tack arms to top of body ¾" from center with hands facing down. Glue porcelain head to top of body between arms.

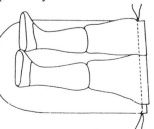

Diagram 1   *Diagram 2*

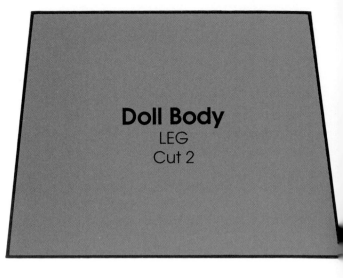

Doll Body
LEG
Cut 2

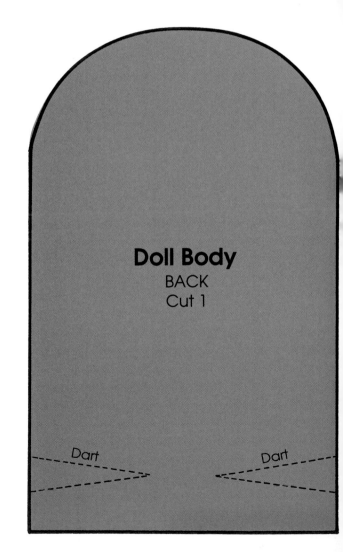

Doll Body
BACK
Cut 1

Dart   Dart

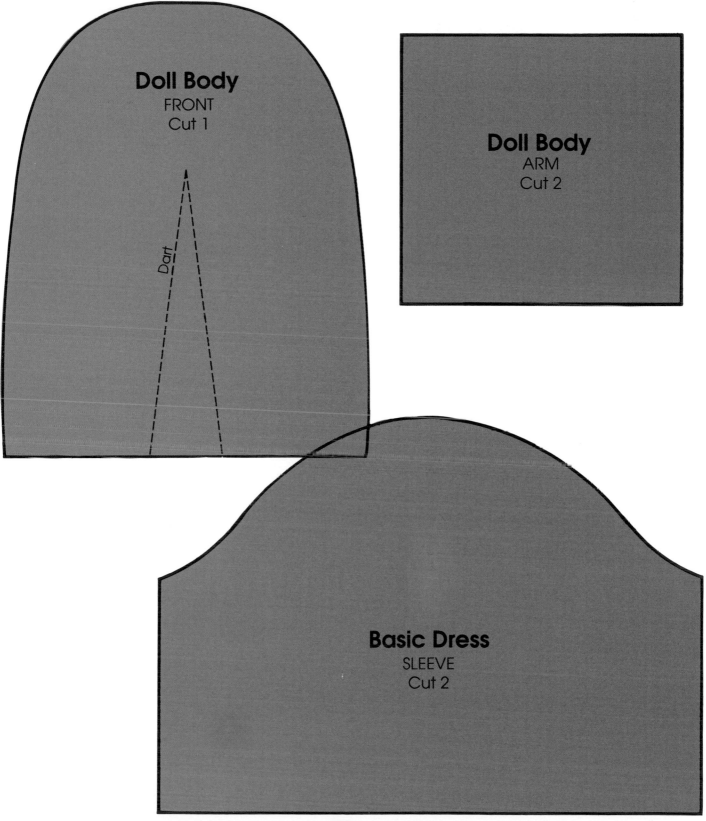

Doll Body
FRONT
Cut 1

Dart

Doll Body
ARM
Cut 2

Basic Dress
SLEEVE
Cut 2

Basic Dress

MATERIALS

¼ yard of 45"-wide fabric; matching thread
6"–8" of elastic thread
Two small snap sets

DIRECTIONS

All seams are ¼".

1. Make Basic Dress patterns, transferring all information. Cut Basic Dress pieces according to patterns. Cut one 27" x 7" piece for skirt.

2. With right sides of one bodice front and two bodice backs facing, stitch shoulders. Repeat for lining.

3. With right sides of bodice and bodice lining facing, match shoulder seams. Stitch up one center back seam, around neck, and down second center back. Clip curved edges. Turn right side out. Proceed to treat both layers of bodice as one layer of fabric.

4. Stitch ⅛" hem in wrist edge of one sleeve. Stitch gathering threads in sleeve cap. Gather sleeve to fit armhole. With right sides facing, stitch sleeve cap to armhole. Repeat for remaining sleeve.

5. Cut two equal lengths of elastic thread, sewing one length ¼" above hem at wrist, either by hand or with a zigzag stitch. With right sides facing, stitch one bodice side seam and one sleeve. Repeat for remaining side seam and sleeve.

6. Fold skirt with right sides facing, matching short ends. Stitch short ends to within 2" of top edge; backstitch. Press seam open. (This seam is center back; long edge with opening will be waist.) Stitch ⅛" hem in edges of opening.

7. Mark center front of skirt at waist. Stitch gathering threads along waist. Stitch ½" hem on lower edge of skirt by hand or machine.

8. Mark center front of bodice at waist. Stitch gathering threads on waist. Gather skirt to fit bodice. With right sides facing, match center of skirt to center of bodice and stitch. Sew snaps on center back opening at neck and waist of dress.

Petticoat

MATERIALS

¼ yard of light-weight fabric; matching thread
28" of 1"-wide lace trim
3" of ⅛"-wide elastic

DIRECTIONS

All seams are ¼".

1. Cut one 27" x 6½" piece from light-weight fabric. Fold with right sides facing to equal 13½" wide. Stitch short ends.

2. Slipstitch trim to one long edge; overlap ends.

3. To make casing, stitch ½" hem on remaining long raw edge, leaving an opening. Thread elastic through casing; overlap ends ½" and secure. Stitch opening closed.

Pantaloons

MATERIALS

⅛ yard of light-weight fabric; matching thread
6"–8" of elastic thread
3" of ⅛"-wide elastic

DIRECTIONS

All seams are ¼".

1. Make Pantaloons pattern, transferring all information. Cut Pantaloons pieces according to pattern.

2. With right sides facing, stitch front to back along center seams. Stitch ⅛" hem in bottom of each leg. Cut two equal lengths of elastic thread, sewing one length ¼" above hem, either by hand or with a zigzag stitch. With right sides facing, fold, aligning center seams. Then stitch inseam.

3. To make casing, stitch ½" hem at waist edge, leaving an opening. Thread elastic through casing; overlap ends ½" and secure. Stitch opening closed.

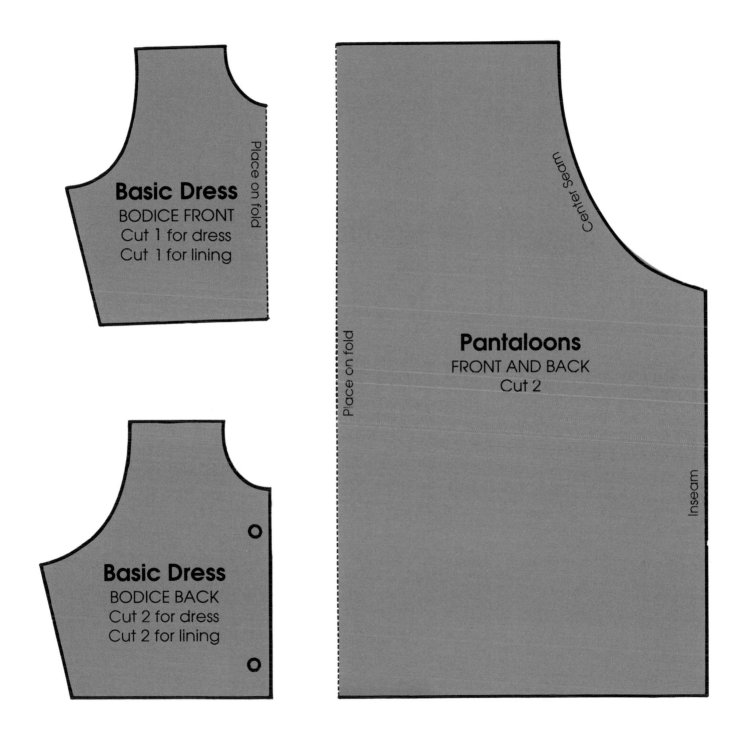

Basic Dress
BODICE FRONT
Cut 1 for dress
Cut 1 for lining

Place on fold

Basic Dress
BODICE BACK
Cut 2 for dress
Cut 2 for lining

Pantaloons
FRONT AND BACK
Cut 2

Place on fold

Center Seam

Inseam

Roses and Bows

Stitched on Waste Canvas 14 over mauve water-marked cotton fabric, the finished design size is 2¾" x ¾" for each motif; stitch ten. Begin stitching topskirt design 5½" from one long edge and 2½" from one short edge. The fabric was cut 32" x 12".

MATERIALS

Completed design piece on Waste Canvas 14 over mauve
   water-marked cotton fabric; matching thread
⅛ yard of unstitched mauve water-marked fabric
⅜" yard of pink polyester-silk fabric; matching thread
⅝ yard of ⅛"-wide white lace trim
1¼ yards of ⅛"-wide green silk ribbon
Two 6"– 8" lengths of elastic thread
Two small snap sets

DIRECTIONS
All seams are ¼".

1. Cut design piece for topskirt to 27" x 7" with bottom edge of design 3" above 27" edge. Make Basic Dress and Pantaloons patterns, transferring all information. From unstitched mauve fabric, cut bodice front and back according to patterns. From pink fabric, cut sleeve and Pantaloons pieces according to patterns, one 27" x 7" piece for skirt and one 4" x 2" piece for collar. Cut one 8" and two 7" lace lengths. Cut six equal ribbon lengths.

2. For collar, sew gathering threads on both 4" edges. Gather one edge to fit neckline of bodice front; baste. Gather opposite edge loosely. Topstitch remaining edges to bodice, parallel to and 1" from neckline, securing gathers. Trim pink fabric very close to topstitching. Gather and stitch 8" lace length to collar over topstitching. Tack one ribbon length to center of collar above lace; tie into a bow.

3. Complete Steps 2–5 of Basic Dress, adding one 7" lace length over hem on each wrist.

4. Complete Step 6 of Basic Dress on design piece and pink skirt piece. Complete Steps 2–3 of Pantaloons.

5. Place wrong side of design piece over right side of pink skirt, matching center back seams and waist edges. Complete Step 7 of Basic Dress, hemming each skirt. Then complete Step 8 of Basic Dress.

6. To make balloon gathers in topskirt, thread both ends of one ribbon length through needle, leaving a loop on end. One half inch below center where two flowers meet, thread ribbon from front to back, looping ribbon under and then over hem of skirt; thread needle through ribbon loop. Tie ends into bow. Repeat for every other flower design.

Anchor		DMC (used for sample)	
		Step 1: Cross-stitch (1 strand)	
892	−	225	Shell Pink-vy. lt.
893	O	224	Shell Pink-lt.
875	△	503	Blue Green-med.
878	✕	501	Blue Green-dk.

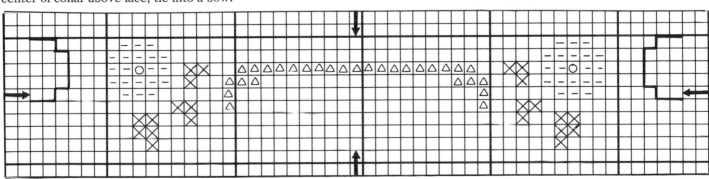

Stitch Count: 39 x 9 (for one motif)

Spring Fancy

Stitched on country Quaker Cloth 28 over two threads, the finished design size is 9⅞" x 1½". Center Jumper skirt design horizontally and begin stitching 2½" from one long edge. The fabric was cut 24" x 10".

MATERIALS

Completed design piece on country Quaker Cloth 28; matching thread
Scrap of unstitched country Quaker Cloth 28
Scrap of tan fabric for lining
⅜ yard of floral print fabric
⅝ yard of cream lace trim
¾ yard of ⅛"-wide mauve silk ribbon
Dressmaker's pen
Large needle
6"–8" of elastic thread
Four small snap sets
One 10" piece of green garland
Assorted dried flowers
Metallic thread
Glue

DIRECTIONS
All seams are ¼".

1. Cut design piece for Jumper skirt to 21" x 6½" with bottom edge of design 1" above 21" edge. Make Basic Dress and Jumper bodice front and bodice back patterns, transferring all information. From unstitched Quaker Cloth, cut one Jumper bodice front and two bodice backs. Cut matching pieces from tan fabric for lining, omitting pin pleat. From floral fabric, cut Basic Dress pieces according to patterns; cut one 27" x 7" piece for skirt. Cut one 8" and two 7" lace lengths. Cut one 12" and three 8" ribbon lengths.

2. To make Jumper, fold Quaker Cloth bodice front with wrong sides matching. Stitch ¼" from, and parallel to, center

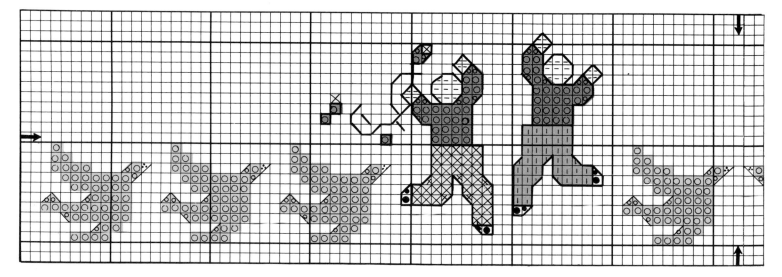

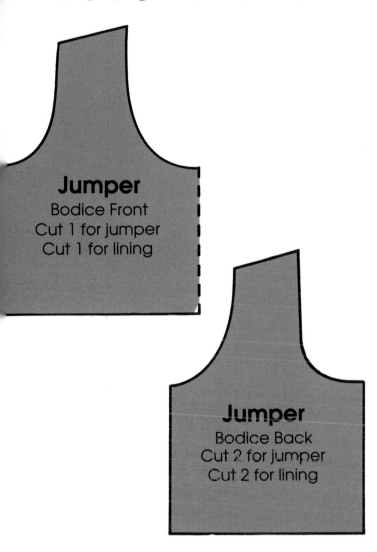

Jumper
Bodice Front
Cut 1 for jumper
Cut 1 for lining

Jumper
Bodice Back
Cut 2 for jumper
Cut 2 for lining

fold. Open bodice front, pressing pin pleat out flat. See Steps 2–3 of Basic Dress to complete jumper bodice.

3. Mark placement for ribbon at ¼" intervals on each side of pin pleat stitching. Thread 12" ribbon length through large needle. Begin stitching behind pin pleat front at upper left mark, leaving a 3" tail of ribbon. When finished lacing, leave a 3" tail on upper right side and tie ends into bow; see photo on page 39.

4. Stitch ¼" hem in short ends of Jumper skirt, either by hand or machine. Complete Steps 7–8 of Basic Dress.

5. To make floral dress, complete Steps 2–8 of Basic Dress. Weave one of each remaining ribbon lengths through lace trim at neckline and wrists of dress.

6. Glue dried flowers to garland and loop metallic thread around entire length. Baste one garland end to each sleeve wrist.

Anchor			DMC (used for sample)	
Step 1: Cross-stitch (2 strands)				
886			677	Old Gold-vy. lt.
881			3779	Terra Cotta-vy. lt.
894			223	Shell Pink med.
110			208	Lavender-vy. dk.
121			793	Cornflower Blue-med.
849			927	Slate Green-med.
862			3362	Pine Green-dk.

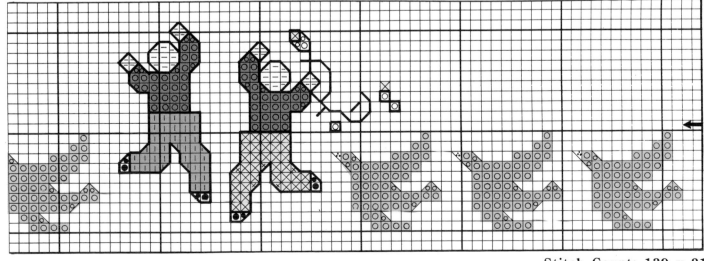

Stitch Count: 139 x 21

Learning the ABCs

Stitched on Waste Canvas 14 over light green fabric, the finished design size is 19⅛" x ⅝" for one repeat of alphabet. Begin stitching skirt design 4½" from one long edge and 2½" from one short edge, leaving two stitches between each letter. The fabric was cut 32" x 12".

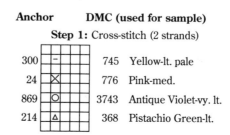

Anchor		DMC (used for sample)	
		Step 1: Cross-stitch (2 strands)	
300	-	745	Yellow-lt. pale
24	X	776	Pink-med.
869	O	3743	Antique Violet-vy. lt.
214	△	368	Pistachio Green-lt.

134

MATERIALS

Completed design piece on Waste Canvas 14 over light green
  fabric; matching thread
⅛ yard of unstitched light green fabric
⅛ yard of light pink fabric
⅛ yard of light-weight white fabric; matching thread
Two 6"–8" lengths of elastic thread
Two 3" lengths of ⅛"-wide elastic
28" of 1"-wide lace trim
1 yard of ⅛"-wide pink silk ribbon
1 yard of ⅛"-wide yellow silk ribbon
1 yard of ⅛"-wide green silk ribbon
1 yard of ⅛"-wide purple silk ribbon
Two small snap sets
Glue

DIRECTIONS
All seams are ¼".

1. Cut design piece to 27" x 7" with bottom edge of design 2"
above 27" edge. Make Basic Dress and Pantaloons patterns,
transferring all information. From unstitched light green
fabric, cut Basic Dress and Pantaloons pieces according to
patterns.

2. Complete Steps 2–3 of Basic Dress. Complete Steps 2–3 of
Pantaloons. Complete Steps 1–3 of Petticoat.

3. Cut one 27" length each of yellow, pink, purple and green
ribbon; set aside. Cut two 2" lengths of yellow ribbon, two
2¼" lengths of purple ribbon and two 2½" lengths of green
ribbon. Fold into loops and pin one length of each color to
each sleeve edge at shoulder seam with fold toward neck,
placing yellow, then purple and green loops together as one.

4. Glue ribbon scraps to bodice front; see photo on page 91.

5. Complete Steps 4–8 of Basic Dress, securing ribbons in
armhole and side seam.

6. With remaining 27" lengths of ribbon, glue pink ribbon
around skirt ¼" above top edge of design. Then glue yellow
ribbon ¼" below bottom edge of design. Glue purple ribbon
½" below design; and green ribbon ¾" below design.

Peachy Peas

Stitched on Waste Canvas 14 over peach-striped fabric, the
finished design size is ⅝" x ⅜" on bib and 3½" x 2⅞" on
apron. Center bib design horizontally and begin stitching
1⅝" from one long edge. Center apron design horizontally
and begin stitching 3½" from one long edge The fabric was
cut 4" x 4" for bib and 25" x 11" for apron.

MATERIALS (for apron)

Completed designs on Waste Canvas 14 over peach-striped
  fabric; matching thread
¼ yard unstitched peach-striped fabric
½ yard peach fabric
⅜" of 1½"-wide white eyelet trim
⅝" of ¾"-wide white eyelet trim
⅝" of ⅛"-wide green silk ribbon
One small snap set

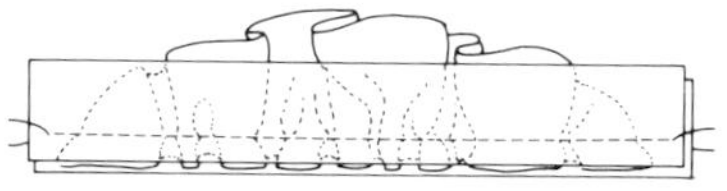

Diagram 1

DIRECTIONS
All seams are ¼".

1. Cut apron design piece to 20" x 6" with bottom edge of
design 1" above 20" edge. Cut bib design piece to 1¾" x 1¾"
with design centered. Make ruffle, Pantaloons and Basic
Dress patterns transferring all information. From unstitched
peach-striped fabric, cut ruffle and Pantaloons pieces
according to patterns; also cut two 7" x 1" strips for waistband, four ¾" x 5½" strap pieces. From peach fabric, cut
Basic Dress pieces.

2. Complete Steps 1–8 of Basic Dress. Complete Steps 1–3
of Pantaloons.

3. Stitch narrow hem in curved edge of each ruffle. Stitch
gathering threads on straight edge of each ruffle and gather
to 5½". Cut two 6" lengths of 1½"-wide eyelet trim. For
each strap, sandwich one ruffle and a 6" length of eyelet trim
between two straps with right sides facing, aligning raw
edges, and with ruffles ¼" from strap ends; see Diagram 1.
Stitch long edge, catching ruffle and trim in seam. Trim
seam allowances. Fold right side out.

4. With right sides facing, stitch bib design piece and lining
across top edge. Turn and press. Cut one 2¼" length of
¾"-wide eyelet trim and one 2¼" length of ribbon. With

eyelet trim behind top edge of bib, and ¼" showing above top edge, tack to bib sides. Slipstitch ribbon across bib ⅛" from top edge.

5. Fold raw edges of strap ¼" to inside. Sandwich one edge of bib between strap pieces, aligning all bottom edges. Topstitch long edge and ends closed. Repeat with remaining strap, securing opposite side of bib.

6. Mark centers of lower bib edge and long edge of each waistband strip. With right sides facing, sandwich bib between strips, matching centers on front. Stitch long edge and short ends; clip corners. Turn waistband.

7. To complete apron, stitch ¼" hem on each short end of apron. Stitch ½" hem on lower edge of apron. Slipstitch ¾"-wide eyelet trim behind hem with ¼" showing below hem. Slipstitch remaining ribbon ⅛" from bottom of design, around bottom edge of apron.

8. Stitch gathering threads in waist of apron. Gather to 5½". Mark center of waist edge. Fold raw edges of waistband under ¼". Sandwich skirt between waistband strips, matching centers. Slipstitch long edge. Tack ends of ruffles to back of waistband. Sew snap set to waistband ends.

Ruffle
Cut 2

Place on fold

Anchor		DMC (used for sample)	
	Step 1: Cross-stitch (2 strands)		
264		472	Avocado Green-ultra lt.
266		471	Avocado Green-vy. lt.

9 x 6 (for bib)

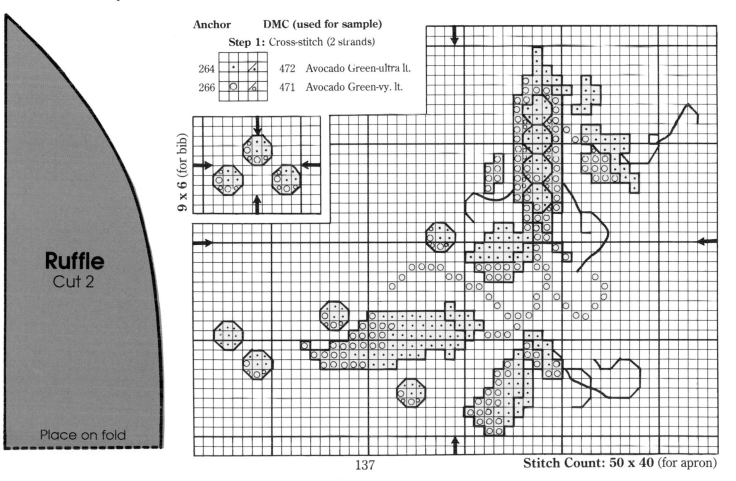

Stitch Count: 50 x 40 (for apron)

Dino Dynamite

Stitched on Waste Canvas 14 over white fabric, the finished design size is 8⅝" x 6⅜". The fabric was cut 32" x 12".

Anchor		DMC (used for sample)	
Step 1: Cross-stitch (2 strands)			
891	O	676	Old Gold-lt.
66	◉	3688	Mauve-med.
69	✕	3687	Mauve
208	·	563	Jade-lt.
210	△	562	Jade-med.
212	✕	561	Jade-vy. dk.
Step 2: Backstitch (1 strand)			
236	⌐	3799	Pewter Gray-vy. dk.
Step 3: French Knot (1 strand)			
236	●	3799	Pewter Gray-vy. dk.

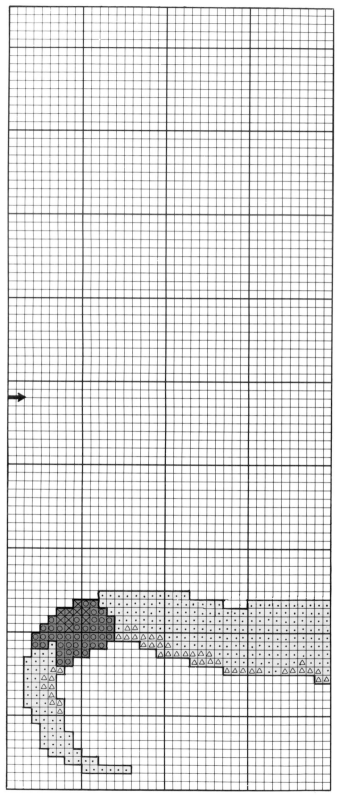

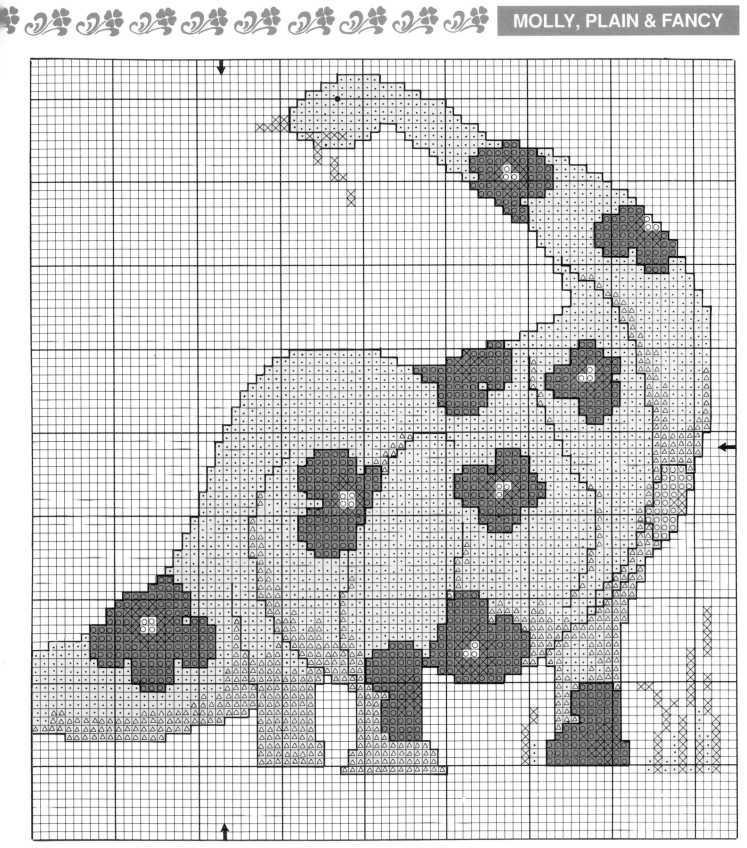

Stitch Count: 120 x 90

MATERIALS

Completed design piece on Waste Canvas 14 over white
   fabric; matching thread
¼ yard of unstitched white fabric
⅛ yard light-weight white fabric; matching thread
Scraps of green fabric for bias
Two small snap sets
6"–8" of elastic thread
28" of 1"–wide lace trim
23" of ⅜"-wide green ribbon

DIRECTIONS
All seams are ¼".

1. Cut design piece for skirt to 27" x 7" with bottom edge of
design 1" above 27" edge. Make Basic Dress and Pantaloons
patterns, transferring all information. From unstitched white
fabric, cut Basic Dress and Pantaloons pieces according to
patterns.

2. Complete Steps 1–3 of Pantaloons. Complete Steps 1–3 of
Petticoat.

3. From green fabric, cut ¾"-wide bias, piecing as needed to
equal two 6" lengths for sleeves, one 4" length for neck and
one 22" length for hem. Complete Steps 2–3 of Basic Dress.

4. With right sides facing, stitch one 6" bias length to each
sleeve on wrist edge. Slipstitch bias to wrong side of each
wrist edge. Stitch gathering threads in each sleeve cap.
Gather sleeves to fit each armhole. With right sides facing,
stitch sleeve cap to bodice. Complete Step 5 of Basic Dress.

5. Fold skirt with right sides facing, matching short ends.
Stitch short ends to within 2" of top edge; backstitch. Press
seam open. (This seam is center back; long edge with opening
will be waist.) Stitch ⅛"hem in edges of opening.

6. Mark center front of skirt at waist. Stitch gathering threads
on waist. With right sides facing, stitch 22" bias length to
bottom edge of skirt. Slipstitch bias to wrong side. Complete
Step 8 of Basic Dress.

7. With right sides facing, stitch 4" bias length on bodice
neckline. Slipstitch bias to wrong side.

8. Clip ends of green ribbon into a "V" and tie around waist.
See photo on page 123.

Country Maid

Stitched on Waste Canvas 14 over blue-striped fabric,
the finished design size is 2⅜" x 2⅛". Center skirt design
horizontally and begin stitching 4" from one long edge.
The fabric was cut 32" x 12".

MATERIALS

Completed design piece on Waste Canvas 14 over
   blue-striped fabric; matching thread
¼ yard of unstitched blue-striped fabric
⅛ yard of light blue fabric
One 12"-wide scrap of light-weight white fabric
2⅜ yards of ⅛"-wide trim
One small snap set
6"–8" of elastic thread

DIRECTIONS
All seams are ¼".

1. Cut design piece to 27" x 7" with bottom edge of design
1½" above 27" edge. Make Basic Dress and Pantaloons
patterns, transferring all information. From unstitched blue-
striped fabric cut Basic Dress pieces according to patterns.

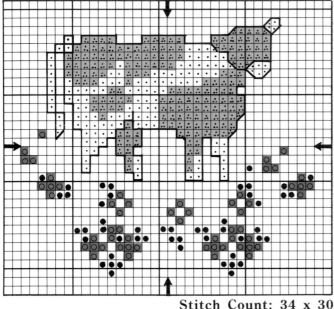

Stitch Count: 34 x 30

Diagram 1

Cut Pantaloons pieces from light blue fabric according to patterns. Cut hip shawl from light-weight white fabric; see Diagram 1. Cut two 4", one 22" and two 27" trim lengths.

2. Stitch two rows of 4" trim ⅛" apart across bodice front, with bottom row 1¼" from bottom edge. Complete Steps 2–5 of Basic Dress.

3. Complete Steps 2–3 of Pantaloons.

4. Stitch two rows of 27" trim ⅛" apart on skirt, with bottom row ¾" from edge. Complete Steps 6–8 of Basic Dress.

5. Measure and mark ½" from each short edge of shawl. Pull horizontal threads in fabric below marks, forming fringe; see Diagram 1. Tie shawl around waist; see photo on page 101.

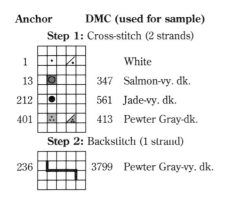

Anchor		DMC (used for sample)	
Step 1: Cross-stitch (2 strands)			
1			White
13		347	Salmon-vy. dk.
212		561	Jade-vy. dk.
401		413	Pewter Gray-dk.
Step 2: Backstitch (1 strand)			
236		3799	Pewter Gray-vy. dk.

General Instructions ⊰
Cross-Stitch Guidelines

Fabrics: Counted cross-stitch is usually worked on even-weave fabric. These fabrics, manufactured specifically for counted thread embroidery, are woven with the same number of vertical and horizontal threads per inch. Because the number of threads in the fabric is equal in each direction, each stitch is the same size. The number of threads per inch in even-weave fabrics determines the finished design size.

Waste Canvas: Waste Canvas is a coarse, fabric-like substance used as a guide for cross-stitching on fabrics other than even-weaves. Cut Waste Canvas 1" larger on all sides than the finished design size. Baste it to the fabric to be stitched. Complete the stitching. Then dampen the stitched area with cold water. Pull the waste canvas threads out one at a time with tweezers. Pull all the threads running in one direction first, then pull out the opposite threads. Allow the stitching to dry. Place face down on towel and iron.

Preparing Fabric: Cut even-weave fabric at least 3" larger on all sides than the design size, or cut it the size specified in instructions. If the item is to be finished into a pillow, for example, the fabric should be cut as directed. A 3" margin is the minimum amount of space that allows for comfortably working the edges of the design. To prevent fraying, whipstitch or machine zigzag raw fabric edges.

Needles: Needles should slip easily through the holes in the fabric, but not pierce the fabric. Use a blunt tapestry needle, size 24 or 26. Never leave a needle in the design area of work. It can leave rust or a permanent impression on fabric.

Floss: All numbers and color names are cross-referenced between Anchor and DMC brands of floss. Cut floss into 18" lengths; longer pieces tend to twist and knot. Run the floss over a damp sponge to straighten. Separate all six strands and use the number of strands called for in the code. If floss is twisted, drop the needle and allow the floss to unwind itself.

Centering the Design: Fold the fabric in half horizontally, then vertically. Place a pin in the fold point to mark the center. Locate the center of the design on the graph by following the vertical and horizontal arrows in the left and bottom margins. Begin stitching all designs at the center point of the graph and the fabric unless the instructions indicate otherwise.

Graphs: Each symbol represents a different color. Make one stitch for each symbol, referring to the code to verify which stitch to use. Use the small arrows in the margins to find the center of the graph. When a graph is continued, the bottom two rows of the graph on the previous page are repeated, separated by a small space, indicating where to connect them. The stitch count is printed with each graph, listing first the width, then the length of the design.

Codes: The code indicates the brand of thread used to stitch the model, as well as the cross-reference for using another brand. The steps in the code identify the stitch to be used and the number of floss strands for that stitch. The symbols match the graph, and give the color number and name for the thread. A symbol under a diagonal line indicates a half cross-stitch. Blended threads are represented on the code and graph with a single symbol, but both color names are listed.

Securing the Floss: Insert your needle up from the underside of the fabric at your starting point. Hold 1" of thread behind the fabric and stitch over it, securing with the first few stitches. To finish thread, run under four or more stitches on the back of the design. Never knot floss unless working on clothing. Another method of securing floss is the waste knot. Knot your floss and insert your needle from the right side of the fabric about 1" from design area. Work several stitches over the thread to secure. Cut off the knot later.

Stitching: For a smooth cross-stitch, use the "push and pull" method. Push the needle straight down and completely through fabric before pulling. Do not pull the thread tightly. Consistent tension throughout ensures even stitches. Make one stitch for every symbol on the chart. To stitch in rows, work from left to right and then back. Half-crosses are used to make a rounded shape. Make the longer stitch in the direction of the slanted line.

Carrying Floss: To carry floss, weave floss under the previously worked stitches on the back. Do not carry thread across any fabric that is not or will not be stitched. Loose threads, especially dark ones, will show through the fabric.

Cleaning Completed Work: When stitching is complete, soak it in cold water with a mild soap for 5–10 minutes; rinse. Roll in a towel to remove excess water. Do not wring. Place work face down on a dry towel and iron on a warm setting until dry.

Stitches

Cross-stitch: Make one cross for each symbol on the chart. Bring needle and thread up at A, down at B, up at C, and down again at D.

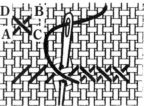

For rows, stitch from left to right, then back. All stitches should lie in the same direction.

Half Cross-stitch: The stitch actually fits three-fourths of the area. Make the longer stitch in the direction of the slanted line on the graph. Bring needle and thread up at A, down at B, up at C and down at D.

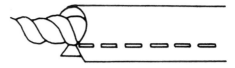

Backstitch: Complete all cross-stitching before working back stitches or other accent stitches. Working from left to right with one strand of floss (unless designated otherwise on code), bring needle and thread up at A, down at B, and up again at C. Go back down at A and continue in this manner.

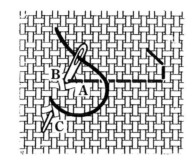

French Knot: Bring the needle up at A, using one strand of embroidery floss. Wrap floss around needle two times (unless indicated otherwise in instructions). Insert needle beside A, pulling floss until it fits snugly around needle. Pull needle through to back.

Sewing Hints

Corded Piping: Center cording on the wrong side of the bias strip and fold the fabric over it, aligning raw edges. Using a zipper foot, stitch through both layers of fabric close to the cording. Trim the seam allowance to ¼".

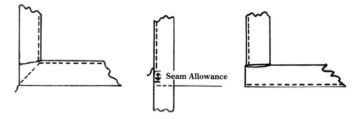

Mitering: To miter a corner, sew border strips up to, but not through, the seam allowance; backstitch. Repeat on all four edges, making stitching lines meet exactly at the corners. Fold two adjacent border pieces together. Mark, then stitch at a 45° angle. Trim seam allowance to ¼".

To miter a binding, stitch the bias to the work with right sides facing, using the seam allowance indicated. Stitch to, but not through, the seam allowance; backstitch. Fold bias at a 90° angle to stitched edge and turn the corner. Resume stitching, meeting the backstitch at the seam allowance. Repeat at each corner. Fold bias to back, turning under seam allowance. Slipstitch, covering stitching line of binding and mitering each corner on both sides of fabric.

Seam Allowance

Suppliers

For a merchant near you, write to the following suppliers:

Murano 30 (*amaretto, cream, ash rose, cracked wheat, moss green*)
Belfast Linen 32 (*white, cream, driftwood*)
Dublin Linen 25 (*white*)
Annabelle 28 (*ice blue*)
Hardanger 22 (*white*)
Floba 25
Rustico 14
Waste Canvas 14
Linda 28 (*dirty linen*)
Quaker Cloth 28 (*country*)
Zweigart Fabrics
2 Riverview Drive
Somerset NJ 08873-1139

Silk Gauze 30
Kreinik Mfg. Co., Inc.
P.O. Box 1966
Parkersburg WV 26102

Wood Boxes
Reed Baxter Woodcrafts Inc.
P.O. Box 2186
Eugene OR 97402

Porcelain Jars
Anne Brinkley Designs Inc.
21 Ransom Road
Newton Centre MA 02159

Jobelan 28 (light blue)
Antique Tan Linen 28
Wichelt Imports, Inc.
Rural Route 1
Stoddard WI 54658

French Rosette Trim
Elsie's Exquisiques
513 Broadway
Niles MI 49120

Sewing Machine
Bernina of America
534 W. Chestnut
Hinsdale IL 60521

Mill Hill Beads
Gay Bowles Sales, Inc.
P.O. Box 1060
Janesville WI 53547

Vanessa-Ann Afghan Weave 18
Wire Gazebo
Molly Porcelain Doll Parts
Chapelle Designers
Box 9252 Newgate Station
Ogden UT 84409

Batting, fleece, polyester stuffing
Fairfield Processing Corporation
88 Rose Hill Avenue
P.O. Drawer 1157
Danbury CT 06810

Glue
Aleene's
85 Industrial Way
Buellton CA 93427

Index

Basic Dress 128
Butterfly Wings 42

Clever Hideaway 19
Counting Dinosaur 110
    Code 116–117
    Graph 112–117
Country Maid 140
Cowpoke Star 120
Cozy Coaster Basket 88

Dino Dynamite 138
Doll Body 126

Enduring Lily 108

Fat Red Hen 118
Framed Fancy 33
Fresh Carrots 86

Garden Gazebo 72
Garden of Letters 6
    Code 14–15
    Graph 8–17
General Instructions 141

Home Tweet Home 83

In My Mother's Garden 60
    Code 66–67
    Graph 62–67

Jewelry Keeper 40

Keeping Secrets 36

Learning the ABCs 134
Little Lights 56
Luminous Roses 22

Magnolia Ladies 44
    Code 52
    Graph 46–51
Meadow Reflections 104
Molly, Plain and Fancy 124

Mother's Favorite Saying 74
    Code 82
    Graph 76–81
Mother's Memories 120

Pantaloons 128
Peachy Peas 136
Petticoat 128
Pocket Full O' Flowers 53
Precious Rose 18
Prissy Pillow 58

Roses and Bows 130
Rose Tray 23

Soft Wings 102
Spring Fancy 132
Suppliers 143

The Peaceful Pasture 92
    Code 94
    Graph 95–100

Wings on Air Afghan 68

You Lift Me Up 26
    Code 32
    Graph 28–33

All of us at Meredith® Press are dedicated to offering you, our customer, the best books we can create. We are particularly concerned that all the instructions for making projects are clear and accurate. Please address your correspondence to Customer Service Department, Meredith® Press, Meredith® Corporation, 150 East 52nd Street, New York, NY 10022.

In My Mother's Garden: An American Sampler is the fifth in a series of cross–stitch books. If you would like the first four books in the series, *The Changing Seasons: An American Sampler; Quilt Designs in Cross–Stitch: An American Sampler 1989; Country Cross–Stitch Designs: An American Sampler 1990; and Home Is Where the Heart Is: An American Sampler*, please write to Better Homes and Gardens Books, P.O. Box 10670, Des Moines, IA 50336, or call 1-800-678-2665.